Important Update

On **September 10, 2025**, the Department of War (DOW) published the **Final Cybersecurity Maturity Model Certification (CMMC) Rule** in the *Federal Register*. This rule, now part of **48 CFR / DFARS**, becomes **effective November 10, 2025**. It represents the most significant shift in cybersecurity requirements for the Defense Industrial Base (DIB) since DFARS 252.204-7012 was issued nearly a decade ago.

The rule makes one thing absolutely clear: cybersecurity is no longer optional. It is a mandatory condition for doing business with the DOW. CMMC is intended to protect the sensitive information that underpins U.S. military operations and technological advantage by ensuring that every contractor—large or small—meets verifiable cybersecurity standards.

Key Provisions in the Final Rule

- Establishes **CMMC Levels 1, 2, and 3**, aligned to NIST standards.
- Requires **annual self-assessments and affirmations** for all contractors.
- Mandates **third-party C3PAO assessments** for most companies handling CUI.
- Assigns **Level 3 assessments** to DOW's DIBCAC for critical programs.
- Uses **SPRS (Supplier Performance Risk System)** for certification tracking.
- Allows limited **conditional certifications** with POA&Ms to close gaps.
- Enforces compliance through **contract eligibility**—no certification, no award.

For defense contractors, this means the countdown has begun. Those who delay may find themselves shut out of opportunities when CMMC clauses begin appearing in contracts.

That is why this *DoW CMMC Everything* book is more valuable than ever. It was created to simplify the complexity of CMMC, explain what the requirements mean in practice, and provide step-by-step guidance for preparing your organization. With this book, you have the tools to move beyond confusion and into compliance—positioning your company to compete, win, and deliver securely in the defense marketplace.

Introduction

The FutureFeed platform was created to enhance our national security by enabling those in and beyond the defense supply chain to create fully managed information security programs compliant not only with legal and regulatory requirements, including NIST SP 800-171, but also with industry best practices. We continue to enhance FutureFeed with new capabilities, including NIST SP 800-171 Revision 3, which will be required by DOW for CMMC in the future and to support the current Canadian Program for Cyber Security Certification (CPCSC).

At the same time, we know even the best tools can only do a portion of the work. That's why we offer built-in training; sponsor the **CS5 – The Official Conference of the Cyber AB** (https://cs5global.org/); and provide a range of helpful webinars and educational options—both online and in person.

It's also why we've written this book. It answers many CUI- and CMMC-related questions and helps you identify additional resources that can support your compliance journey.

To keep learning, join the **FutureFeed Explorers Webinar Series**—free, practical sessions open to all. Register here: https://futurefeed.co/explorers/

If conversation with others on the same path sounds helpful, we invite you to our weekly **15 Minutes with FutureFeed** sessions. These are open to all and cover a wide range of topics including CUI, CMMC, NIST SP 800-171, cybersecurity, compliance, and the FutureFeed platform. To register, visit: https://FutureFeed.co/15.

Prefer a one-on-one? Email us at **Sales@FutureFeed.co** ›r schedule time at https://FutureFeed.co/demo

Good luck on your CMMC journey! If you haven't yet, be sure to reach out to find out how FutureFeed helps take the stress out of compliance.

Mark Berman
CEO, FutureFeed

CMMC Ecosystem Overview

From start to finish, CMMC Level 2 journey can take 12-18+ months. The CMMC Ecosystem is ready to accelerate your CMMC journey.

CMMC Ecosystem by the Numbers

Ecosystem Role	Organizations and People	Sept 2025
Help You Prepare	Registered Provider Organizations (RPOs)	**351**
	Registered Practitioners (RPs)	**1,865**
	Registered Practitioners (Advanced) (RPAs)	**227**
Assess and Certify	Authorized CMMC 3rd Party Assessment Organizations (C3PAOs)	**81**
	Certified CMMC Professionals (CCPs)	**1,039**
	Certified CMMC Assessors (CCAs)	**496**

Getting Help and Staying Up to Date

This book describes how to start building a CMMC compliance program. If your organization needs help getting started or pushing your CMMC compliance program across the finish line, we recommend reaching out to one of our over 200 FutureFeed partners. For a list of our partners and their locations and capabilities, visit our website at https://FutureFeed.co/.

We publish this book in both eBook and printed forms. The eBook version, which we maintain more regularly, can be downloaded from our website.

Contents

The information in this book is not intended to provide, nor does it provide, legal or business advice. Instead, this book provides a high-level overview of certain topics. To help keep the information applicable and accessible to a broad range of readers, generalizations are made that might impact any implementation decisions. Readers should always consult with a competent attorney or other advisor before following any of the advice in this book.

All writing, opinions, and purported statements of fact are solely from and due to the authors' personal experience and research. Readers should not construe any statements contained herein to be from or endorsed/approved by the United States Department of War, The CMMC Accreditation Body (Cyber AB), or any other entity. All writing and statements are the sole responsibility of the authors.

Although the authors have made every effort to ensure that the information in this book was correct at press time, neither Continuous Compliance nor the authors assume, and all parties hereby disclaim, any and all liability to any party for any loss, damage, or disruption caused by any errors or omissions in this book, whether such errors or omissions result from negligence, accident, or any other cause.

Edition 2025.10a

Edition History:
Edition 2025.10a – Revised to align with 48 CFR Part 204 and the CAP
Edition 2025.03a – Revised to align with 32 CFR Part 170
Edition 2024.11b – Corrected dates in Table 6 to show 1-year progression
Edition 2024.11a – Revised to align with CMMC v.2.13
Edition 2024.02a – Initial Version

Building a CMMC Compliance Program

How do I Create a CMMC Compliance Program?

Creating a **Cybersecurity Maturity Model Certification (CMMC)** Compliance program is not an overnight process, and sometimes it can be easy to get distracted as you continue your journey. Following the twelve basic steps illustrated in Figure I, below, can help you stay on the path to success.

Figure I

In the next few pages, we will walk through some of the basic concepts associated with each step.

1 Decide: DIY or Get Help

Decide: DIY or Get Help

The first step in your CMMC journey is deciding whether to implement the requirements yourself or seek outside assistance. Some requirements—such as policy enforcement, user behavior, and accountability—must be owned and executed internally. However, many qualified consultants and service providers are available to support your efforts, easing the burden and guiding implementation.

If you're technically proficient and resourced, you may be able to implement many requirements independently. The CMMC Information Institute has published a list of requirements that are commonly managed in-house and those which are more efficiently outsourced.

If you plan to go it alone, don't make assumptions. There is no "close enough." The 110 controls in NIST 800-171 Rev 2 are recondite; the 320 assessment objectives on which they are graded are precisely defined with little wiggle room. If you decide to do everything yourself, then educate yourself. Take advantage of industry conferences like those sponsored by the Cyber AB and other credible organizations. Use the resources listed in the Key CMMC Tools and Resources section toward the end of this book. Attend webinars. Educate yourself, and don't be afraid to ask for help from the many qualified resources within the CMMC ecosystem.

If you decide to seek help, there are several routes:

- **Consultants** who specialize in CMMC readiness
- **Managed Service Providers (MSPs)** and **Managed Security Service Providers (MSSPs)** who provide IT and security services designed for the Defense Industrial Base
- **Cloud Service Providers (CSPs)** offering platforms with built-in security aligned with CMMC requirements

For cloud services handling CUI, ensure the provider is **Federal Risk and Authorization Management Program (FedRAMP)** authorized at the Moderate impact level or can demonstrate equivalent security in accordance with **Defense Federal Acquisition Supplement (DFARS** clause 252.204-7012 sections (c)-(g). FedRAMP and FedRAMP equivalency are discussed in a later section of this book.

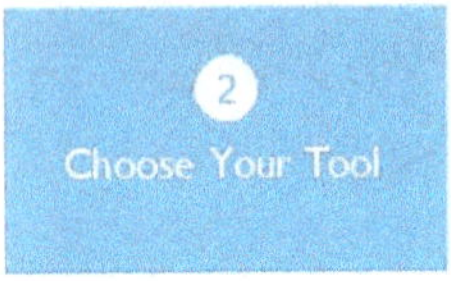

Choose Your Tool

Once you've decided whether to get help or go it alone, the next step is determining how you'll collect and organize the evidence (such as policies, screenshots, logs, etc.) and information needed for your compliance program. There are a wide range of options:

- Spreadsheets
- File folders
- Databases
- OneNote
- Online tools like FutureFeed

Each option has its own strengths and weaknesses.

For very small organizations (1–5 employees), spreadsheets and file folders may be perfectly adequate. These organizations likely have only a handful of assets (e.g., people, equipment, locations) involved in storing, processing (handling), or transmitting the government's information. Spreadsheets are especially attractive because free templates are available, such as the one from the CMMC Information Institute which can help guide your efforts.

Organizations with more employees and assets may benefit from using a more robust tool, such as the FutureFeed platform. These tools streamline and automate many of the tasks described in the next ten steps. While there are fees associated with them, they often accelerate the compliance process enough to pay for themselves in time saved.

There's no one-size-fits-all—what matters is that your system is consistent, secure, and accessible when it's time for an assessment.

3 Find the FCI and CUI

Find the FCI and CUI

At its core, CMMC ensures that Federal Contract Information (FCI) and Controlled Unclassified Information (CUI) are properly safeguarded. In this book, we'll refer to both collectively as **sensitive information**.

To determine whether you're properly safeguarding sensitive information, you first need to know what you have. That means conducting a basic information inventory.

This inventory should identify not only what sensitive information you have, but also:

- Where the information currently resides
- Where it came from (e.g., a prime contractor, another subcontractor, a government agency)
- How it entered the organization (e.g., via email, removable media, secure file transfer)
- In what form(s) it is stored, processed, or transmitted (e.g., paper, email, encrypted files)
- How it moves through the organization (e.g., who accesses it and why)
- How it leaves the organization (e.g., secure transfer, removable media, email)

While you're at it, don't just look for government-related sensitive information. Your environment may also include other types of regulated or sensitive data—like personnel records, payment card data, healthcare records, student records, client data, vendor or partner intellectual property, and your own company's proprietary information.

If you handle any of this other information, it's important to identify the safeguarding requirements that apply. For example, a contract involving third-party intellectual property may contain its own protection clauses. If you handle credit card transactions, the **Payment Card Industry Data Security Standard (PCI DSS)** applies.

Although this book focuses on CMMC compliance, the same foundational inventory practices apply across many other compliance frameworks.

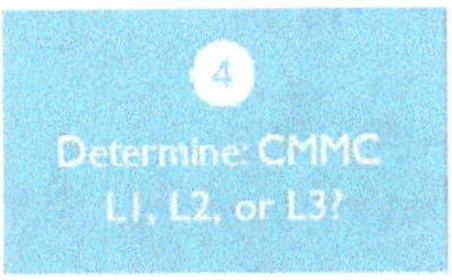

Determine: CMMC Level 1, 2, or 3

As a DOW contractor, you need to determine the requirements that must be included in your compliance program. The list of requirements will inherently include those in CMMC.

If you only handle FCI, then you should only need to comply with the CMMC Level 1 requirements.

If you handle CUI, you must comply with not only the CMMC Level 1 requirements for your assets that handle FCI, but also the CMMC Level 2 requirements for your assets that handle CUI. These are generally defined as the 110 requirements in the **National Institute of Standards and Technology (NIST) Special Publication (SP)** 800-171 Rev. 2, as assessed against the 320 Assessment Objectives in NIST SP 800-171A.

If you are a prime contractor on a critical **United States Department of War (DOW)** program, DOW has indicated that you will need to not only earn a third-party certification of compliance with the CMMC Level 2 requirements, but you must also comply with the CMMC Level 3's twenty-four (24) requirements from NIST SP 800-172 (see 32 CFR 170.14 for the list) and earn a separate certification of compliance with those requirements from DOW's **Defense Industrial Base**

Cybersecurity Assessment Center (DIBCAC). DIBCAC will assess you using the corresponding Assessment Objectives defined in NIST SP 800-172A.

According to DOW, contracts will require a Level 3 Certification if they involve mission-critical or breakthrough technology, and the CUI requires extra protection beyond Level 2. Specific triggers that would cause a contract to require a Level 3 Certification are: advanced or unique military technologies; situations where a single data breach could harm multiple DOW systems (ubiquity); and large-scale aggregated CUI in one system (volume risk).

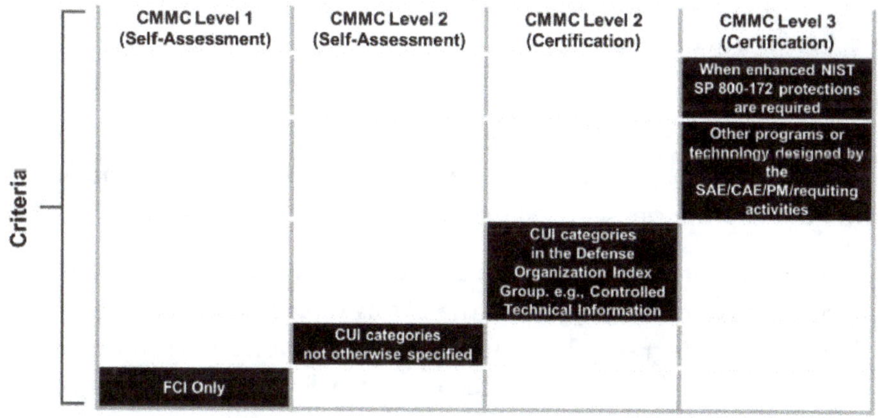

CAE: Component Acquisition Executive
CUI: Controlled Unclassified Information
FCI: Federal Contract Information
PM: Program Manager
SAE: Service Acquisition Executive

If you handle CUI Specified, you will also need to comply with the requirements defined in the corresponding **law, regulation, or government-wide policy (LRGWP)** that is the basis for the CUI designation.

In addition, you should be aware of the requirements in DFARS 252.204-7012(c)-(g). These include incident reporting requirements, the use of only FedRAMP Moderate Authorized (or equivalent) cloud services, and more. While these requirements are technically not part of NIST SP 800-171, a CMMC assessment team is likely to expect that your **System Security Plan (SSP)** describes how you are meeting these requirements.

Please note that all incidents involving CUI must be reported to DOW via DOW's DIBNET portal. The registration process that must be followed to gain access to the DIBNET portal can take longer than the 72-hour mandatory reporting timeline specified in DFARS 252.204- 7012. Therefore, your organization is strongly encouraged to take the time **NOW** to create at least two accounts (a primary and a backup) who have access to the DIBNET portal.

5
Establish an SSP Framework

Establish an SSP Framework

Although not technically required in CMMC Level 1, it is a good practice to begin creating an SSP. The SSP defines the requirements you need to meet and how you meet them.

If you are using a tool like FutureFeed, this will likely be done automatically for you. If you are using a spreadsheet, some will help you create an SSP, and in other cases you will want to use an SSP template like the one published by NIST.

Regardless of whether it is created automatically for you or if you have to create it yourself, the goal of the SSP is to create a structured cybersecurity program. The effort you put into it now will make your organization significantly more secure and will make maintaining that level of security much easier.

6
Inventory Your Assets

Inventory Your Assets

In addition to the basic information inventory, when it comes to a CMMC assessment, you will also need to know:

- **People:** Who has access to the relevant FCI or CUI, and why do they need access?
- **Places:** Where is the FCI or CUI stored, processed, or transmitted (e.g., offices, data centers, etc.)?
- **Technology:** What hardware, software, and other technology is used to store, process, or transmit the FCI or CUI?

- **Processes:** What documentation (e.g., policies, procedures, plans, drawings, etc.) do you have that helps describe how you are safeguarding the FCI or CUI?

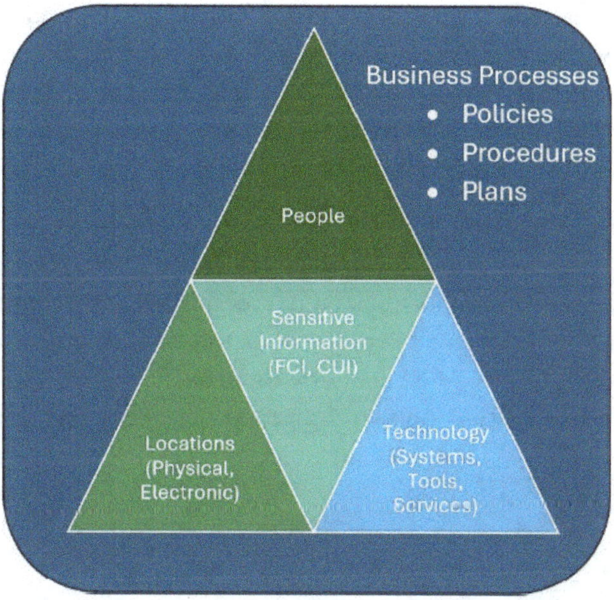

Figure 2

If you do not have any CUI but you would like to become a government contractor who is authorized to handle CUI, you should build your program based on the type(s) of CUI you expect to handle. Your prime contractor or a government representative, like a Contracting Officer or Program/Project Manager, and even an Apex Accelerator, can help you identify this.

7 Define Current and Desired Scope

Define Current and Desired Scope

Once you have completed the data inventory and identified the corresponding requirements, the next step is to determine the "scope" of the environment to be assessed.

For many small businesses this will be the entire company's network. However, for companies with more than 15-20 employees, it may be more economically efficient and secure to compartmentalize the government's information (especially CUI) into a secure "**enclave**," or separate IT environment.

The CMMC Scoping Guides have additional details on how to establish scope. In a nutshell, if the contractor is handling CUI and the contractor wants to position a piece of equipment, a person, a physical location, or another "**asset**" so that it is "**out of scope**" and not subject to CMMC compliance requirements, the contractor must physically or logically isolate the assets that handle CUI from those which do not.

For example, in a building, this means that CUI must be stored, processed, or transmitted in rooms with appropriate physical access controls that prevent unauthorized persons from accessing the CUI. In a network, this means that equipment handling CUI must be on separate, dedicated VLANs, subnets, or networks with appropriate controls in place so that only authorized equipment and users can access the CUI.

8
Identify Gaps and Create POA&Ms

Identify Gaps and Create POA&Ms

Now that you know what is "in scope" for your compliance review, the next step is to compare your in-scope assets and information against the various requirements. When it comes to assessing CMMC compliance, be sure your assessment includes not only the requirements in NIST SP 800-171, but also the objectives in NIST SP 800-171A. In a platform like FutureFeed, this is handled automatically for you. Some spreadsheets and other free resources that are available online only help you track compliance at the requirement level, which is not sufficient for CMMC certification purposes.

The goal of this "**gap assessment**" is to identify the gaps between what you are doing now and what you are expected to do under the corresponding law, regulation, government-wide policy, contractual requirement, etc. At this stage, it is important to be honest and self-critical as you evaluate your compliance. When in doubt, you should err on the side of marking yourself as noncompliant.

At the same time, be sure to not dwell on things that are missing. If a gap is identified, simply make a record of the gap and move on. Do not bother trying to remediate things, even if it is only the creation of a minor piece of documentation, at this stage of the game.

Most companies identify between 200 and 300 gaps in their programs when they conduct their first gap assessment. If you are like them, you will probably make significant changes to your information security program that may cause you to rethink things anyway, so any remediation efforts at this early stage will probably be of limited value and will likely wind up being redone.

If your organization meets a particular requirement, you should record that fact in the SSP, including a description of how the organization meets the requirement. If you have evidence, such as policies, drawings, screen captures, log files, etc. that help prove that the requirement is met, they should be noted in the SSP as well. This helps you build a "traceability matrix" that allows any third-party, such as an assessor or auditor, to understand the organization's compliance with the requirements.

Without the traceability matrix, the assessor would, in theory, have to comb through every document you create trying to find the needle in the haystack that proves your compliance. Most assessors won't spend that much time on your assessment; they will likely fail you instead. We will talk about evidence in more detail in steps 9 and 10.

If you are not familiar with NIST SP 800-171 or CMMC, we recommend that you do not conduct your gap assessment in the order in which the requirements appear in those documents. This is because, quite frankly, some of the requirements in the Access Control family (the first set of requirements in NIST SP 800-171) can be difficult to understand. Starting with them can make the process feel daunting and will be discouraging. Instead, we recommend working through the families in the following order:

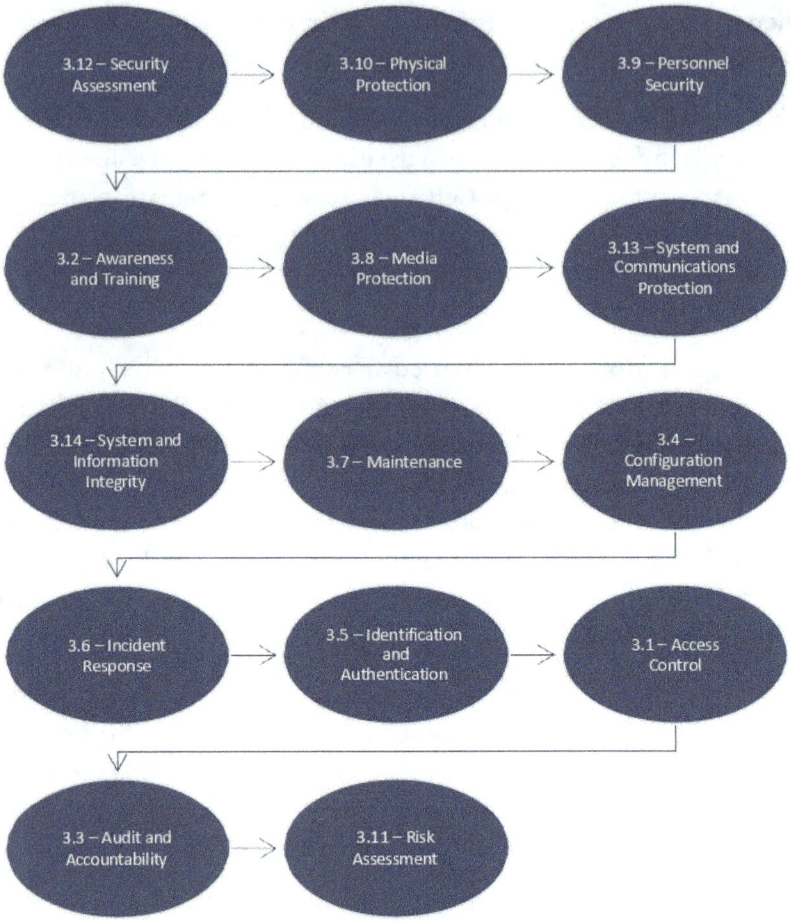

Figure 3

With a good sense for the gaps in your information security program, the next step is to create a remediation plan. To do this, you should create a Plan of Action & Milestone(s) (**POA&M**), for each gap you identified. The POA&M should include:

- a description of what needs to be done (your "plan of action),
- one or more milestones that align with the plan of action,
- the person/people who will be involved in closing the POA&M, and
- financial commitments from the company to ensure that the POA&M is closed.

In many cases, since the remediation of one gap may allow another to also be remediated, it may be more efficient to group the POA&Ms into projects. Grouping POA&Ms into projects also makes it easier to prioritize the remediation activities and manage the remediation process. It also makes it much easier for management to oversee the remediation process.

Close POA&Ms

After the POA&Ms and projects are created, the next step is to begin the remediation process. As you remediate, your goal should be to not only meet the requirement, but also to document the business practice(s) implemented by your organization that allow it to meet the requirement.

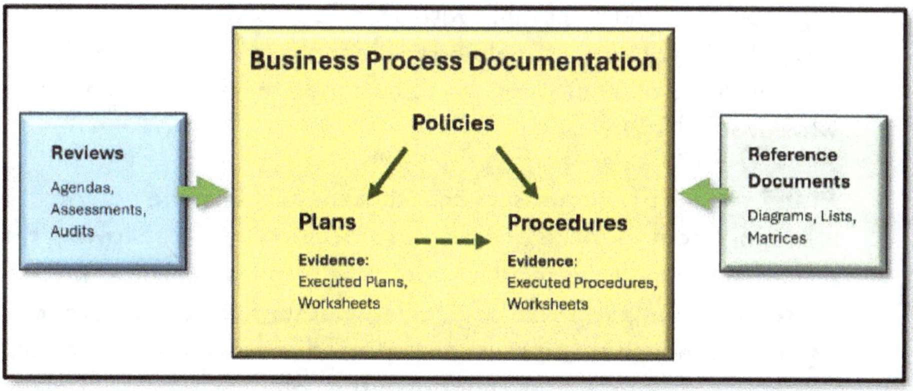

Figure 4

In general, practices are comprised of policies, procedures, plans, and the corresponding evidence. It is helpful to understand the differences between these types of documents.

- **Policies** are high-level statements that describe how the organization intends to meet a particular requirement. For example, an employee off boarding policy might include language like: "All accounts associated with a terminated employee must be disabled within four (4) hours of the employee's termination. The

Director of HR shall notify the CISO as promptly as possible, and not more than thirty (30) minutes, after the termination of an individual's employment with the company. The CISO shall ensure that all accounts associated with the terminated employee are deactivated within three (3) hours of receipt of the termination notification from the Director of HR."

- **Procedures** are step-by-step instructions that guide the responsible party through the process of meeting the company's intent as described in a policy. Procedures are generally like recipes; they yield the same results each time they are followed. For example, an employee off boarding procedure may include instructions which guide the reader (e.g., a system administrator) through the process of logging into Microsoft 365 and deactivating a terminated employee's account, and how to report the completion of that process to the CISO. In some cases, several procedures might be required to comply with a single policy. When writing procedures, your goal should be to write them with sufficient detail that junior-level employees can follow them without guidance wherever possible.

- **Plans** are like procedures, except that they require the person following them to make one or more decisions while following the plan. For example, an incident response plan may require the person executing the plan to decide whether a particular event is significant enough that it must be reported to law enforcement and regulators, or whether to shut down the company's entire IT systems. Since these decisions can have significant consequences for the organization, the execution of a plan is often reserved for management-level employees.

- **Evidence** demonstrates that the policies, procedures, and plans are followed as part of the organization's normal course of business. If the organization does not collect evidence, proving compliance with the organization's policies, as well as the broader legal and regulatory requirements the policies address, will be exceedingly difficult. Evidence can take many forms, including screen captures of system configurations, copies of procedures signed off by the responsible employee that demonstrates that the procedure was followed, and worksheets that are signed off by the responsible employee which document the steps taken by the employee while executing a plan.

As you craft your compliance program and are considering the evidence that it will create, it will likely be helpful to understand the three types of evidence an assessment team will expect to see: Examine, Interview, and Test. While the assessment team may not request every type of evidence for every requirement, your implementation team should be prepared to offer all three types wherever practical and relevant.

- **Examine** – This is comprised of documents that can be reviewed as part of the early phases of the assessment. The assessment team will review the documents to understand the scope of the assessment and how the organization expects to meet the various requirements.

- **Interview** – Once the assessment team has reviewed the documentation, they will interview members of your organization (including your IT or External Service Providers, where applicable). The goal of the interview is to ensure that the day-to-day work that is performed is consistent with the documentation. For example, if the organization's password policy requires all passwords to be at least 12 characters long and, during the interview, a member of your team who is responsible for configuring password policies says that passwords need only be 8 characters long, that could create issues.

- **Test** – Assuming the documentation and interview are in alignment, the assessment team may also ask your team to demonstrate how the requirement is met in your live environment. For example, you may be asked to open Microsoft 365 (or another, similar tool deployed in your environment) to prove that the password complexity settings are consistent with the policy.

As noted in the discussion around Step 8, the SSP should also include a traceability matrix. A traceability matrix helps the assessment team easily identify which practices your organization considers relevant for a particular requirement or objective. This allows the assessment team to more easily review the practices to ensure they align with the requirements.

Validate

With the gaps closed and a comprehensive program in place, it might seem as though it is time to call in a **CMMC 3rd Party Assessment Organization (C3PAO)** to assess your organization. However, we recommend making one more pass through the SSP and requirements. We're all human, and often mistakes are made, or actions are taken that were only meant to be temporary but then are forgotten about. Making one last "validation" pass through the requirements help ensure all the "i"s are dotted and "t"s are crossed before you engage the C3PAO.

Certify

The next step in this process is to engage an authorized C3PAO to conduct a formal assessment of your compliance with the requirements. Be sure to only select a C3PAO who is currently listed in the Cyber AB's Marketplace as an authorized C3PAO.

If the assessment is successful, the C3PAO will issue a certificate of compliance to you and record that certificate with DOW.

Maintain

The last step in the process is to maintain your environment's compliance with the requirements. As discussed in more detail below, although CMMC certifications are valid for three years, an Affirming Official must affirm their organization's continued compliance in the off years.

Why should I use a tool like FutureFeed as Part of My Compliance Program?

You can conduct, store, and maintain your information and other inventories directly in the FutureFeed platform. Unlike spreadsheet-based tools, FutureFeed automatically builds your SSP and POA&Ms for you as you conduct the gap assessment. You can use the built-in project management capabilities to track the completion of POA&Ms and projects.

As you work, the FutureFeed platform calculates your SPRS score in real time, and the automated dashboards and deliverables make it easy for everyone to track the organization's progress. FutureFeed also allows you to easily organize and store your evidence, including new evidence and evidence of continuous compliance.

In short FutureFeed accelerates the creation of your CMMC compliance program. Visit **https://FutureFeed.co** for more information and to schedule a demonstration!

Where can I learn more?

The remainder of this book provides insight into the CMMC program, including its structure, status, and history. It also identifies issues to be mindful of, and techniques for avoiding them, that will be beneficial as you build out your compliance program. The book is also full of links to external sources of information that can help you with your CMMC journey.

CMMC:
the 50,000 Foot View

Does CMMC apply to all government information?

Technically, no. CMMC does not apply to information which the government makes publicly available, nor does it apply to classified information. As a practical matter, however, CMMC will apply to most of the information DOW contractors create or receive under a contract with DOW.

How does CMMC help ensure the safeguarding of FCI and CUI?

Under the CMMC program, DOW contractors are required to review their information security programs against certain requirements to ensure that the programs meet (i.e., comply with) those requirements. A senior-level representative of the organization, referred to as an **Affirming Official**, is required to submit affirmations of continued compliance with the requirements on an annual basis.

In addition, most contractors storing, processing, or transmitting CUI will be required to have an authorized C3PAO conduct an assessment of the contractor's information security program and certify that the program meets the published requirements. These certifications are valid for three years.

CMMC Model

	Model	Assessment
LEVEL 3	**134** requirements based on NIST SP 800-171 & 800-172	Government-led assessment every 3 years & annual affirmation
LEVEL 2	**110** requirements aligned with NIST SP 800-171	Third-party assessment every 3 years & annual affirmation; self-assessment every 3 years & annual affirmation for select programs
LEVEL 1	**15** requirements	Annual self-assessment & annual affirmation

Figure 5

When is an organization subject to a given CMMC level?

As Figure 5, above, illustrates, CMMC is comprised of three levels.

CMMC Level 1 applies to all DOW contractors. All DOW contractors are required to implement the fifteen (15) information security requirements defined in FAR 52.204-21. All DOW contractors must conduct a self-assessment (referred to as "**Level 1 (Self)**") and submit an affirmation to DOW that they have properly and completely implemented the requirements in FAR 52.204-21. As illustrated in Table 1, below, DOW estimates that nearly 2/3 of its contractors will only need to meet the Level 1 (Self) requirements.

There is one exception to the Level 1 (Self) requirement. Where the contractor a) also handles CUI, and b) the "scope" of the people, tools, processes, and facilities that handle the FCI and CUI are **exactly** the same, then the contractor's CMMC Level 2 (Self), CMMC Level 2 (C3PAO), or CMMC Level 3 (DIBCAC) assessment will be sufficient.

CMMC Level 2 applies to all DOW contractors who handle CUI. As will be discussed in more detail below, DOW is rolling out CMMC in 4 phases. During Phase 1 of the CMMC implementation, only CMMC Level 2 (Self) status is required. In Phases 2 and beyond, most DOW contractors will be required to obtain third-party certifications of their compliance with the requirements in NIST SP 800-171 before the contractors can be awarded, or participate in, a contract.

As illustrated in Table 1, below, after CMMC Phase 1 is complete, only 5,000 of the 83,085 contractors expected to handle CUI will be able to self-certify compliance with NIST SP 800-171. Most organizations that handle, or expect to handle, CUI are likely better off assuming that they will need a CMMC Level 2 (C3PAO) assessment and certification.

CMMC Level 3: According to DOW, contracts will require a Level 3 Certification if they involve mission-critical or breakthrough technology, and the CUI requires extra protection beyond Level 2. Specific triggers that would cause a contract to require a Level 3 Certification are: advanced or unique military technologies; situations where a single data breach could harm multiple DOW systems (ubiquity); and large-scale aggregated CUI in one system (volume risk). In addition to earning a CMMC Level 2 (C3PAO) status and certification, these contractors must also undergo an audit by DOW's DIBCAC team to validate that the contractor has implemented twenty-four (24) specific requirements from NIST SP 800-172.

CMMC Assessment Type	Estimated Number of Contractors [1]	% of Total Contractors
CMMC Level 1 (Self)	209,540	62%
CMMC Level 2 (Self)	4,596	2%
CMMC Level 2 (C3PAO)	118,289	35%
CMMC Level 3 (DIBCAC)	2,298	1%

Table 1

What is the relationship between FCI, CUI, CMMC, and NIST SP 800-171, NIST SP 800-171A, and the CMMC Assessment Guides?

The CMMC program was created to ensure FCI and CUI are properly safeguarded by government contractors. FAR 52.204-21 establishes the fifteen basic safeguarding requirements that all contractors who handle FCI (which is essentially all contractors) must meet.

For each of the requirements, the CMMC Assessment Guide Level 1 draws one or more "assessment objectives" from correlated portions of NIST SP 800-171A as the basis for determining whether a particular requirement is met. Contractors should ensure that they are meeting the requirements **and the objectives** defined in the CMMC Assessment Guide Level 1 before they submit an affirmation of compliance.

The CUI Program establishes the requirements in NIST SP 800-171 as the minimum protections that must be in place to safeguard CUI in contractor information systems. It also establishes NIST SP 800-171A as the assessment guide for determining whether the requirements in NIST SP 800-171 have been met. The CMMC Assessment Guide Level 2 provides additional details and clarifications about DOW's

[1] Contractor counts drawn from Tables 16, 19, 22, and 25 of 32 CFR 170.

interpretation of certain requirements. However, NIST SP 800-171A is the authoritative assessment guide that must be used by federal agencies (and C3PAOs) when evaluating contractor compliance with NIST SP 800-171.

When a contractor performs a CMMC Level 2 (Self) assessment, and when a C3PAO's assessment team performs a CMMC Level 2 (C3PAO) assessment, the assessment must not only be conducted against the 110 requirements defined in NIST SP 800-171, that assessment must also be conducted against all of the applicable Assessment Objectives associated with each requirement in NIST SP 800-171A.

When can contractors begin earning a CMMC Level 2 (C3PAO) status and certification?

C3PAOs and DIBCAC conducted **Joint Surveillance Voluntary Assessments (JSVAs)** for over a year before the December 16, 2024, effective date of the 32 CFR CMMC rule. Companies that successfully completed their JSVAs and which earned a perfect 110 score were awarded CMMC Level 2 (C3PAO) status and a certification from the C3PAO in early 2025.

C3PAOs were authorized to begin conducting formal CMMC certification assessments in January 2025. As of September 1, 2025:

- 270 FINAL CMMC Level 2 Certificates have been issued
- 9 CONDITIONAL CCMC Level 2 Certificates have been issued
- 91 CMMC Level 2 Assessment were in progress

When will CMMC certifications be required?

32 CFR 170 indicates that there is a 4-phase roll-out for CMMC.

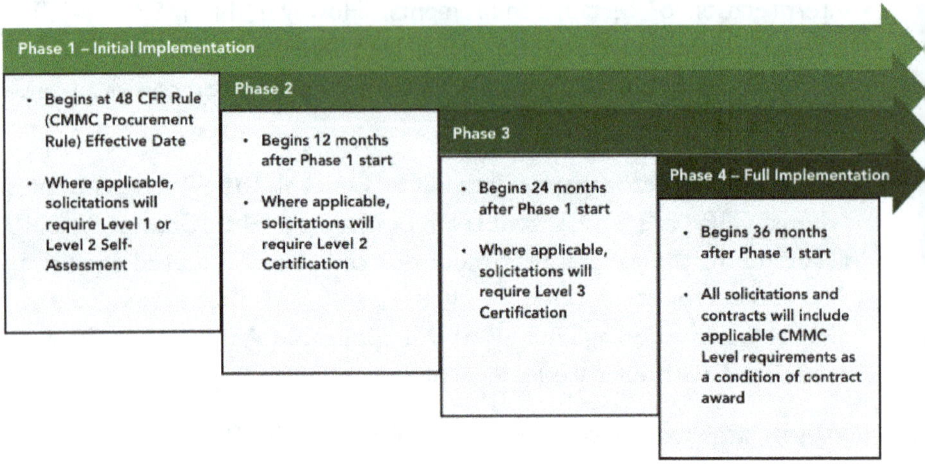

Phase	Start Date	Requirement:	PMO Approval Required
1	Nov. 10, 2025	Level 1 (Self) or Level 2 (Self) requirements in all applicable DOW solicitations and contracts.	Yes
2	Nov. 10, 2026	Phase 1 + Level 2 (C3PAO) requirements in all applicable DOW solicitations and contracts.	Yes
3	Nov. 10, 2027	Phase 2 + Level 3 (C3PAO) requirements in all applicable DOW solicitations and contracts. Level 2 (C3PAO) required to exercise option period.	Yes
4	Nov. 10, 2028	Full implementation of CMMC Program requirements in all DOW solicitations and contracts including option periods.	No

Figure 6

The dates provided in Figure 6, above, are based on the November 1, 2025, effective date of the 48 CFR CMMC Final Rule.

It should be noted that DOW reserves the right to begin including CMMC Level 2 (C3PAO) status and certification requirements during Phase 1. During Phase 2, DOW may accelerate the CMMC Level 3 (DIBCAC) status and certification requirements in certain contracts and may delay the CMMC Level 3 (C3PAO) status and certification requirements until an option year in certain contracts. During Phase 3, DOW may delay the CMMC Level 3 (DIBCAC) status and certification requirement until an option year in certain contracts.

Where can I learn more about CMMC?

The CMMC regulations can be found in the **Code of Federal Regulations (CFR)**. They are often referenced by the name of the CFR volume in which they appear, such as the FAR or DFARS. The most up to date, official versions of the CMMC guidance documents (e.g., the CMMC Assessment and Scoping Guides) can be found on the DoD CIO website.

The website of the Cyber AB, the DOW-authorized organization which is responsible for managing the CMMC ecosystem, has useful information about CMMC and the various entities and individual certifications that exist in the ecosystem.

The book "*CMMC Simplified*" by Fernando Machado offers a high-level overview of the CMMC program and is a great resource for those new to CMMC. The book "*The Guide to Everything CMMC*" by Tara Lemieux provides detailed walk-through of each NIST SP 800-171 requirement and a description of what assessors are typically expecting to see when they review each requirement.

CMMC-Related Business Considerations

Do we have to get ready for CMMC by ourselves?

In a word, no.

What does it cost to implement a CMMC-compliant information security program?

The enforcement of NIST 800-171 through the CMMC program effectively makes the DIB a regulated industry, according to Summit 7 CEO Scott Edwards[2]. Companies in regulated industries necessarily spend more on IT, information security, and compliance. And it's not just the cost of building a compliant security program; it's also the on-going cost of operating the program.

The cost to your organizations to implement a CMMC program is influenced by a variety of factors including:

- the CMMC level you need to meet;
- your organization's cyber maturity and current state of compliance (your SPRS score);
- the types of security tools and business processes your organization already has in place;
- the number of people and devices that need access to the sensitive information;
- whether your organization can leverage an "enclave" solution or if the government's sensitive information must be accessible to the majority of the people and/or devices in your organization;
- the level of management support, resource availability, and willingness to accept short-term business impacts as business processes are, and IT infrastructure is, changed; and,
- whether your organization has the internal expertise to install, configure, document, and manage everything internally or if you will need outside support.

Given the significant influence of these factors, the cost to implement a CMMC-compliant information security program can vary greatly. Summit 7 estimated the one-time cost of achieving compliance and the ongoing annual cost of maintaining compliance by extrapolating

[2] CUI-CON 2025, *Budgeting for CMMC*

from the DOW's estimate to implement NIST 800-53[3] (a subset of controls from which the NIST 800-171 controls were selected):

Estimated Cost to Implement and Maintain a
CMMC Level 2 Compliant Information Security Program

Cost Range	Term
$175,000 - $265,000	One-Time
$50,000 - $127,000	Annual

Table 2

Based on our conversations with our partners and clients, we have put together the estimated costs in Table 3 for a small (<20 employee) business to implement a CMMC Level 1 compliant information security program in their organization. This is offered only as a starting point, and we want to again stress that there are a variety of factors that will likely impact the total implementation cost for any organization.

Small Business CMMC Implementation Cost	Technology	Consulting
Level 1	$10,000-$20,000	$10,000-$20,000

Table 3

Not included in the prior cost estimates is the cost of the CMMC assessment, which is addressed below. No estimated cost to implement Level 3 has been included. No data are available yet from companies that have needed to address Level 3.

What does a CMMC certification assessment cost?

As with implementation costs, the cost for a third-party to perform a certification assessment will vary based on several factors, including:

[3] SumITUp Podcast / YouTube: Estimating the Cost of NIST 800-171

- the CMMC level;
- the number of physical locations that must be assessed;
- the number, type(s), and certification status of External Service Providers (ESPs) used by the organization; and,
- the complexity of the organization's information security program.

At CMMC Level 3, DIBCAC does not charge the contractor for conducting the assessment or issuing the certification. Therefore, the cost is $0. However, those contractors who must meet the CMMC Level 3 requirements must already have earned a CMMC Level 2 (C3PAO) status and certification, meaning they have still made a significant investment in their information security program.

At CMMC Level 2, given the significant influence the factors outlined above can have on cost, many C3PAOs are reluctant to give cost estimates until after they have had the opportunity to review the contractor's **System Security Plan (SSP)** and other documentation. This, of course, makes it difficult for organizations to budget for the cost of an assessment.

Based on our conversations with C3PAOs, we have put together the estimated costs of a C3PAO assessment for businesses of varying size and complexity.

Third-party Certification Assessment	Cost Range
Level 2 (Large / Complex Businesses)	$100,000 +
Level 2 (Small and Medium Size Businesses / Moderately Complex)	$60,000 - $100,000
Level 2 (Small Business / Cloud and VDI Environment)	$30,000 - $60,000
Level 3 (DIBCAC)	No charge for the Level 3 component

Table 4

The costs listed above are an increase over earlier estimates due to subtle but critical changes that are required under the final CMMC Program Rule.

In the final CMMC Program Rule[4], DOW added a requirement that assessment teams must be comprised of at least one **Lead Assessor**, and at least one **CMMC Certified Assessor (CCA).** Lead Assessors need significantly more education and experience than CCAs, which will likely result in higher billing rates for them. Also, the addition of a 2nd CCA to the team will result in significantly higher costs for the assessment.

Many C3PAOs have expressed disappointment in this approach as they had been trying to find ways to decrease the assessment costs for their clients. Since these assessment team requirements are mandated in 32 CFR 170, the C3PAOs have little flexibility at this time.

Does the government provide or fund any tools or other resources that can help us?

The government offers a range of resources and government-funded programs that may be of interest to you. For example, the Cybersecurity Collaboration Center (C3) at the **National Security Agency (NSA)** offers a **Protective Domain Name System (PDNS)**, vulnerability scanning, threat intelligence collaboration, and automated penetration testing services at no cost to DOW contractors. The United States Air Force's Blue Cyber program has created a series of cybersecurity training videos and handouts that help contractors understand their requirements.

NIST also funds the **Manufacturing Extension Partnership (MEP) National Network**. There are MEPs in each state, and they are tasked with helping ensure US manufacturing companies are competitive at the international level. MEP is a public-private partnership, designed from inception as a cost-share program. Federal appropriations pay one-half, with the balance for each Center funded by state / local governments and/or private entities, plus client fees. Several MEPs across the nation, including TechSolve in Ohio, and the Georgia and

[4] See 32 CFR 170.19(b)(2)

Maryland MEPs, have been actively involved in the CMMC program since its early days, and they can be excellent resources.

Are there any nonprofit organizations or other free resources that can help us understand CMMC better?

Yes. There are nonprofit organizations, like the CMMC Information Institute, which publish low and no cost tools and resources for contractors. The SCORE Association offers mentorship programs through which your business can gain access to cybersecurity coaches who can help your business understand and implement the requirements in NIST SP 800-171 and CMMC. FutureFeed's 15 Minutes with FutureFeed is a free program which enables those on their CMMC journey to share information and gain access to information from trusted industry experts.

Is there funding available to help organizations with their CMMC journey?

Currently, DOW is not providing any direct funding for contractors, and we do not expect that to change. Many organizations have already found alternative funding sources or distributed the cost of meeting the NIST SP 800-171 requirements over multiple years. In the past, DOW has stated that any efforts by DOW to offer assistance for those who waited, despite DOW's admonitions since 2016 to get started on this process, would essentially punish, rather than reward, those who have already complied.

That being said, some industry groups and educational organizations are encouraging Congress to provide low-cost funding, tax breaks, and other incentives to government contractors and other entities as they seek to enhance their cybersecurity programs.

In the interim, your local **Small Business Administration (SBA)** office may also be able to provide recommendations for local funding resources There are also organizations like Parabilis which can help contractors secure funding needed to improve their information security programs.

The Cyber AB and CAICO

The Cyber AB and the CAICO are at the core of the CMMC ecosystem. The Cyber AB, formally the Cybersecurity Maturity Model Certification Accreditation Body, is an independent, nonprofit organization created to implement and oversee the CMMC accreditation process.

The CAICO, formally the Cybersecurity Assessor and Instructor Certification Organization, is a subsidiary of the Cyber AB, responsible for managing the training, examination, and certification of professionals within the CMMC ecosystem. The CAICO ensures that assessors and instructors possess the necessary qualifications and adhere to the standards established to maintain the integrity and quality of CMMC assessments.

The Cyber AB?

The Cyber AB:

- Evaluates and accredits C3PAO to ensure assessments are conducted impartially and in alignment with DOW standards.
- Develops and maintains policies related to the CMMC program
- Serves as the primary liaison between the DOW, defense contractors, and other stakeholders.
- Oversees the Cyber AB Marketplace.
- Offers educational resources to help organizations and professionals stay informed about evolving cybersecurity threats.

The CAICO

The CAICO:

- Develops curricula and examination protocols for CMMC assessors and instructors.
- Oversees relationships with Licensed Publishing Partners (LPPs) and Licensed Training Providers (LTPs), which are responsible for creating and delivering CMMC training materials and courses.
- Directs the creation, validation, and administration of CMMC professional certification exams for assessors and instructors.

The Cyber AB Marketplace

The Cyber AB Marketplace is a centralized online directory designed to connect defense contractors with accredited CMMC service providers. It connects organizations seeking certification with accredited C3PAOs, Registered Provider Organizations (RPOs), Licensed Training Providers (LTPs), and other essential service providers

The marketplace includes the following categories of accredited entities:

- Certified Third-Party Assessment Organizations (C3PAOs)
- Registered Provider Organizations (RPOs)
- Licensed Training Providers (LTPs)
- Licensed Publishing Partners (LPPs)

CMMC Implementation Help

Are there any "easy buttons" when it comes to CMMC Level 2 or Level 3?

Two ways to reduce the effort to meet the NIST SP 800-171 requirements and to obtain a CMMC Level 2 (C3PAO) or Level 3 (DIBCAC) status and certification are enclaving and limiting access to IT systems to only a **Virtual Desktop Interface (VDI)**.

Enclaving can reduce or minimize scope by limiting where CUI is stored, processed, or transmitted. An enclave is a defined boundary within an organization's environment that isolates systems, personnel, and processes handling CUI. The purpose of creating an enclave is to minimize the scope of the CMMC assessment, simplify compliance efforts, and concentrate security controls around the most sensitive areas of the organization.

Without an enclave, the entire organization may be in scope of the assessment, including systems and people that have nothing to do with CUI.

Creating an enclave may require making changes to business processes. An enclave includes not only IT systems (Servers, endpoints, applications, and cloud services that handle and protect CUI), it also includes the individuals within the organization who have access to CUI and facilities where CUI is accessed or stored.

There are several vendors whose products or services can be used to create secure IT enclaves, including Microsoft, AWS, PreVeil, Summit7, RimStorm, Wise Technical Innovations, Kiteworks, Beryllium CuickTrac, C3 Integrated Solutions, and others.

Leveraging a purpose-built enclave can significantly shorten implementation times as compared to modifying an organization's existing infrastructure. To further streamline the implementation timeline, an organization could also consider whether a VDI-based solution would be advantageous.

VDI is a technology that allows employees to access a desktop computer environment remotely. When an individual logs into a VDI session, their physical device is not doing the work. Instead, using only the keyboard and display, they're viewing and interacting with a virtual computer that lives on a central server; the local device simply displaying what's happening in the virtual desktop.

Because data and applications remain in the centralized environment, the physical device is not in scope. CUI never resides on individual laptops; it stays in the secure virtual environment. Under 32 CFR 170.19(c)(1) and 32 CFR 170.19(d)(1), as long as the end-user's computer hosting the VDI client is configured to not allow any processing, storage, or transmission of FCI or CUI beyond the Keyboard/Video/Mouse signals sent to the VDI client, the end-user's computer is considered out-of-scope

This results in fewer devices and fewer systems that are within scope, which directly reduces the time and cost of compliance efforts.

Using a purpose-built enclave and accessing it via a VDI client can drastically reduce the number of assets that must be managed and which are in scope for the assessment. This, in turn, can significantly shorten the implementation and assessment times.

What is an External Service Provider?

An ESP is an intentionally broad term that includes any external people, technology, or facilities providing managed IT or cybersecurity-related services to a DOW contractor, such as **Managed IT Services Providers (MSPs)**, **Managed Security Services Providers (MSSPs)**, consultants, and even **Cloud Service Providers (CSPs)** where those service providers handle CUI or **Security Protection Data (SPD)**.

SPD is data stored or processed by **Security Protection Assets (SPA)** that are used to protect a contractor's assessed environment. SPD is security relevant information and includes but is not limited to: configuration data required to operate an SPA, log files generated by or ingested by an SPA, data related to the configuration or vulnerability status of in-scope assets, and passwords that grant access to the in-scope environment.

What services does an MSP typically offer?

An MSP provides managed **information technology (IT)** services to its clients. These services generally focus on acquiring and maintaining the client's IT infrastructure and ensuring everything runs efficiently. Examples of services MSPs provide include installing and maintaining software, answering end user support questions, fixing/replacing computer equipment, and deploying and managing the client's network.

What services does an MSSP typically offer?

An MSSP provides managed security services. These services generally focus on securing the client's information technology infrastructure. Examples of services provided by MSSPs include performing vulnerability scans of the client's equipment to identify issues that could be exploited by attackers, ensuring that client IT systems are securely configured and have the latest security fixes in place, monitoring the client's IT environment for malicious activity, and responding to any identified malicious activity.

What services does a consultant typically offer?

A consultant typically offers higher-level reviews and analytical services to their clients. These services generally focus on the structure and operation of the client's IT and cybersecurity programs rather than implementation of those programs. Examples of services consultants provide include conducting gap assessments, reviewing and optimizing business practices, drafting and reviewing policies, and creating and managing remediation plans.

Are these differences between MSPs, MSP, and consultants well-established?

No. The descriptions above are generalizations. Clients are increasingly pressuring MSPs to provide security-related services as part of their overall package, and many MSSPs also offer consulting services, meaning that the lines between MSPs, MSSPs, and consultants are often blurred.

This can be advantageous for some contractors in that they can rely on a single ESP to help them with many aspects of their CMMC journey. The fact that only a single entity is involved can significantly reduce the cost. Other contractors find that by ensuring the MSP, MSSP, and consultant roles are handled independently, especially across different ESPs, they gain increased confidence in the resulting programs.

What services do CSPs offer?

This is one of the more difficult answers in this entire book, because CSPs offer a wide range of services. In CMMC, DOW defines a cloud service provider as "an external company that provides cloud services based on cloud computing. Cloud computing is a model for enabling ubiquitous, convenient, on-demand network access to a shared pool of configurable computing resources (e.g., networks, servers, storage, applications, and services) that can be rapidly provisioned and released with minimal management effort or service provider interaction."

Put more simply, cloud computing provides a client with on-demand access to software, platform, and/or compute resources. Examples of these cloud capabilities include **Infrastructure-as-a-Service (IaaS)**, such as the offerings from AWS, Microsoft Azure, and Google Cloud; **Platform-as-a-Service (PaaS)**, such as Salesforce Lightning, Azure App Service, AWS Lambda, and Google App Engine; and **Software-as-a-Service (SaaS)** offerings such as FutureFeed, QuickBooks Online, or HubSpot.

Leveraging a CSP can allow your organization to transfer some of the day-to-day responsibilities to a third party. Figure 7, below, provides a high-level comparison of the responsibilities assumed by different types of CSPs.

For the purposes of clarity, the information in Figure 7 is not the equivalent of a **Customer Responsibility Matrix (CRM)**. CRMs are discussed in more detail below. CRMs must address each requirement and Assessment Objective appropriate to the contractor's CMMC level.

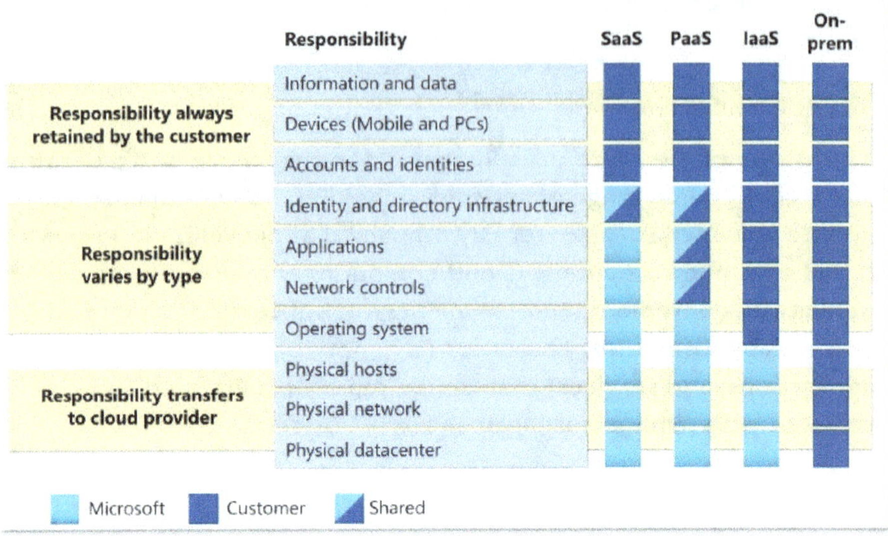

Figure 7

What should I look for when selecting an External Service Provider?

There are many new ESPs entering the market who only have limited experience with or knowledge of CMMC. While some of them may do an excellent job, we recommend looking for ESPs that have been active in the CMMC ecosystem for a significant period and who offer trusted, accurate information.

If you have difficulty determining whether a particular ESP has experience in the CMMC ecosystem, or if you are having difficulty picking between ESPs, we recommend evaluating potential ESPs against these factors:

1. **Proven Experience (MSP/MSSP/Consultant):** Has the ESP helped other clients successfully obtain their CMMC Level 2 (C3PAO) or CMMC Level 3 (DIBCAC) status and certification?

   A clear way to identify a solid resource is to use one that has already proven their ability to deliver at least one successful CMMC Level 2 (C3PAO) or Level 3 (DIBCAC) status and certification for their clients. Some ESPs may even have gained relevant experience as part of a JSVA.

2. **Proven Experience (CSPs):** Have any clients used the CSP's service as part of obtaining their CMMC Level 2 (C3PAO) or CMMC Level 3 (DIBCAC) status?

   As an **Organization Seeking Certification (OSC)**, the last thing a contractor wants is to go through all the motions of creating a CMMC program only to learn that their choice of cloud service prevents them from earning their CMMC Level 2 or Level 3 status. One easy way to feel confident in your choice of CSPs is to use a CSP that has already successfully been used by others as part of their CMMC certification assessment. For example, the FutureFeed platform was successfully used by several OSCs during the JSVA and DIBCAC High assessments, and also by multiple C3PAOs as part of their own DIBCAC assessments.

3. **Eating their own Dogfood:** Has the ESP earned (or do they plan to earn) a CMMC certification, **FedRAMP Authority to Operate (ATO)** or FedRAMP equivalency?

   One of the best ways to gain experience with NIST SP 800-171 and CMMC is to implement the requirements yourself and to live with them on an ongoing basis. This is true for OSCs and ESPs.

   An easy way to identify ESPs who have been through the process is to ask for a copy of their **Customer Responsibility Matrix (CRM)**. This is a document that outlines which of the NIST SP 800-171 requirements the ESP is committing to meet on their own, which ones they will help you meet, and which ones are purely your responsibility. ESPs who are familiar with CMMC and FedRAMP will likely either have a CRM ready to go or will be working on building one.

   Some CSPs publish their CRMs for their clients as documents in the FutureFeed platform. This streamlines the CRM acquisition process for clients of those CSPs.

In addition, some MSPs/MSSPs have implemented their CRM directly in FutureFeed by leveraging the platform's built-in RACI (Responsible, Accountable, Consulted, Informed) tracking capabilities. This makes it very easy for clients of those MSPs/MSSPs to easily identify the individual objectives for which the ESP has taken responsibility.

4. **Commitment:** For MSPs, MSSPs, and Consultants, what level of commitment has the ESP made to establish their role in the CMMC Ecosystem?

   While there are many MSPs, MSSPs, and consultants that have been working with NIST SP 800-171 for many years, it can be difficult to differentiate them from other, more recent entrants to the CMMC Ecosystem. This makes it hard for a contractor to identify an organization they can trust.

   That is why the Cyber AB created the **Registered Provider Organization (RPO)** program. RPOs must make a significant financial investment to become part of that program, and they make a commitment to the Cyber AB that they will abide the Cyber AB's Code of Ethics. Loss of the RPO status will likely have a significant impact on the ESP's business. Therefore, it can be a good indicator of the ESP's role in the CMMC Ecosystem.

   It should be noted that membership in the RPO program is not as relevant to, or particularly appropriate for, organizations that are only acting as CSPs.

5. **Training:** What level of CMMC-related training has the ESP's staff undergone?

   While there are many excellent practitioners who are highly experienced in NIST SP 800-171 and CMMC, it can be difficult to identify them from others who simply talk a good game. The fact that an ESP has on staff one or more Certified **CMMC Instructor (CCI)**, **Certified CMMC Assessors (CCA)**, **Certified CMMC Professionals (CCP)**, or **Registered Practitioners (RP)** is evidence of the ESP's strong investment in ensuring that their services will meet your needs.

Generally, CCIs have more training than CCAs who have more training than CCPs who have more training than RPs, but all have undergone at least some level of training to become familiar with the CMMC requirements.

6. **Using FutureFeed:** Is the ESP using FutureFeed to help them deliver services to you more efficiently and effectively?

   The FutureFeed platform helps organizations create and manage structured information security programs. Although it is very powerful for our end clients, it is especially valuable to ESPs when they deliver their services at scale. The FutureFeed platform helps them onboard clients quicker, identify and remediate gaps more efficiently, and streamlines their ability to support end clients not only during an assessment but also long after. The FutureFeed platform also puts all of the necessary information at your Affirming's Official's fingertips, streamlining the annual affirmation process.

Can any External Service Providers provide complete (i.e. 100%) CMMC services?

No, and you should be very wary of any organization that claims that it can. There are, inherently, certain requirements that only your organization can meet.

For example, the very first objective in NIST SP 800-171A, 3.1.1[a] requires your organization to identify all authorized users for systems that handle CUI. A third party can help you add and remove accounts from those systems, but the third party does not know whether a particular account belongs to someone who is authorized to access CUI. Only your organization can make that determination.

By our count there are at least 83 objectives in NIST SP 800-171A that require at least significant participation by you.

Does an ESP need any special certification?

It depends on the services they provide and the information they handle.

CSPs handling CUI – If the ESP is a cloud service provider and they handle CUI, then the ESP must have a FedRAMP Moderate ATO or the equivalent. You can find a list of FedRAMP authorized CSPs on the FedRAMP Marketplace. Be sure to not merely rely on the presence of an ESP on the FedRAMP Marketplace; you must carefully review the listing to ensure that:

- It corresponds to the specific service you are using, since some CSPs offer both commercial and government/contractor versions of their services, and often only the government/contractor versions have earned a FedRAMP ATO;
- It has a Status of FedRAMP Authorized, not merely FedRAMP Ready or In Process, since FedRAMP Ready and In Process are not equivalent to an ATO; and,
- The Authorization is for at least the Moderate Impact Level.

However, it should be noted that to even be considered for an ATO, the ESP must be a government contractor. Many ESPs do not serve government clients. This makes it effectively impossible for them to obtain an ATO. That is where FedRAMP Moderate equivalency comes into play.

FedRAMP Moderate equivalency has been the subject of significant debate and discussion in the CMMC Ecosystem. In January 2024, DOW published a memorandum defining FedRAMP Moderate equivalency.
However, that memorandum was inconsistent with information in the 32 CFR 170 proposed rule that DOW published only a few days prior. In the public comments that accompany the 32 CFR 170 final rule, DOW indicated that a new FedRAMP Equivalency memorandum is forthcoming.

Until DOW publishes the revised memorandum, if you are leveraging a CSP to handle CUI and that CSP does not have a FedRAMP Moderate (or higher) ATO, it would be wise to discuss with that CSP how they expect to address the FedRAMP Moderate equivalency requirement. Ideally, the CSP should be able to at least provide a letter of attestation from an authorized **FedRAMP 3rd Party Assessment Organization (3PAO)** that states that, in the 3PAO's professional opinion, the CSP's services meet the requirements for an ATO without any changes. If theCSP has not heard of FedRAMP or if they insist that they already meet the requirements but are not listed on the FedRAMP Marketplace and cannot provide any third-party validation that they meet the requirements, it would probably be wise to begin exploring other options.

Other ESPs handling CUI – If the ESP is not a CSP and will be handling CUI (e.g., backups containing CUI are stored by the ESP at their facility):

- The use of the ESP, its relationship to your organization, and the services provided by the ESP must be documented in your SSP;
- The ESP must provide a service description and CRM which describes your and the ESP's responsibilities with respect to the services provided;
- The ESP's services will be assessed within the scope of your assessment against all CMMC Level 2 or Level 3 security requirements (as appropriate); and,
- Any of your on-premises infrastructure that connects to the ESP's product or service offering is part of the assessment scope (i.e., it will be assessed).

ESPs handling only Security Protection Data – If the ESP handles SPD but not CUI, the services provided by the ESP are in scope for the assessment and will be assessed as Security Protection Assets, meaning that they will be assessed against the NIST SP 800-171 requirements that are relevant to the services provided by that ESP.

Note that an ESP that is not a CSP but which handles CUI or SPD may voluntarily undergo a CMMC certification assessment to reduce the ESP's effort required during your assessment. To be effective, the CMMC Level associated with the ESP's CMMC certification must be equal to or greater than your desired or required CMMC Level.

ESPs that do not handle SPD or CUI – If a service provider does not handle SPD or CUI, the service provider does not meet the definition of an ESP and is not in scope for your assessment.

CMMC Assessment Process (The CAP)

Overview of the CMMC Assessment Process

The **CMMC Assessment Process (CAP)** is the standardized framework used to evaluate whether an Organization Seeking Certification (OSC) has implemented the cybersecurity practices required under **NIST SP 800-171** and the **Cybersecurity Maturity Model Certification (CMMC)** program. The CAP is designed to ensure consistency and fairness, so that assessments yield reliable results regardless of which accredited C3PAO (CMMC Third-Party Assessment Organization) or assessment team performs the review. Its purpose is to protect the integrity of CMMC assessments by providing a uniform process that balances thoroughness, objectivity, and efficiency.

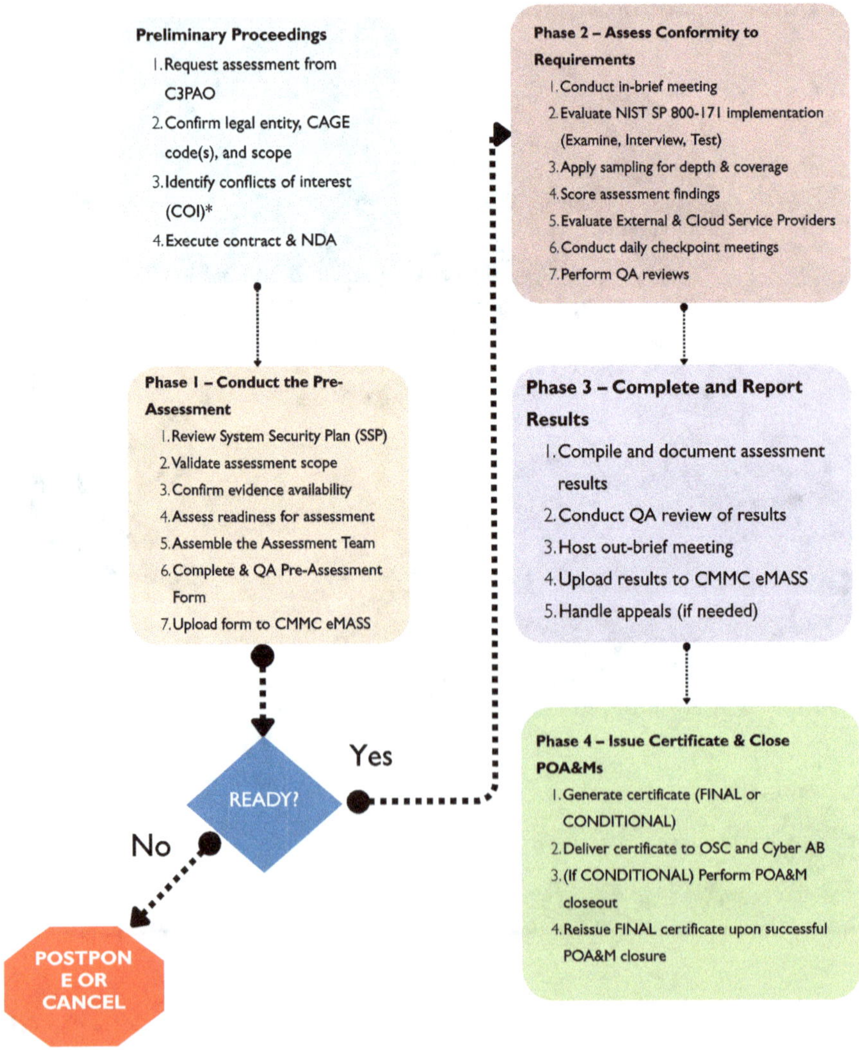

The CAP begins with preliminary proceedings, in which the OSC and its chosen **C3PAO** define the scope, establish contracts, and confirm readiness.

From there, the assessment moves into four structured phases:

- **Phase 1 (Pre-Assessment):** Typically two weeks, focuses on reviewing the System Security Plan (SSP), validating scope, and ensuring evidence is available.
- **Phase 2 (Assessment of Requirements):** Often spans about three weeks, is the heart of the process—assessors examine documents, interview personnel, test systems, and score results against the 110 NIST SP 800-171 practices.
- **Phase 3 (Reporting)**: Usually two weeks, compiles findings into a formal report, includes quality assurance review, and presents results in an out-brief meeting.
- **Phase 4 (Certification and POA&M Closeout)**: May take around three weeks, issues either a Final or Conditional Certificate and closes out any remaining corrective actions.

This structure ensures fairness, accuracy, and repeatability. For executives, the CAP serves as both a compliance mechanism and a trust-building process that validates an organization's ability to protect sensitive information.

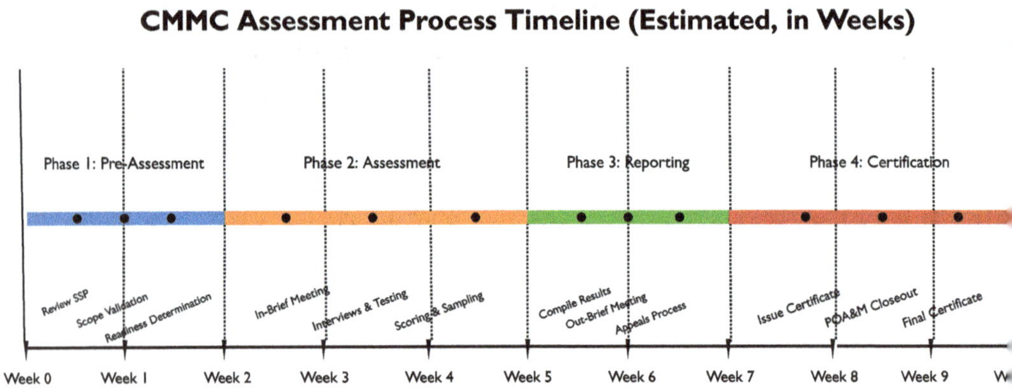
CMMC Assessment Process Timeline (Estimated, in Weeks)
Phase 1: Pre-Assessment
Phase 2: Assessment
Phase 3: Reporting
Phase 4: Certification
Review SSP
Scope Validation
Readiness Determination
In-Brief Meeting
Interviews & Testing
Scoring & Sampling
Compile Results
Out-Brief Meeting
Appeals Process
Issue Certificate
POA&M Closeout
Final Certificate
Week 0
Week 1
Week 2
Week 3
Week 4
Week 5
Week 6
Week 7
Week 8
Week 9

Altogether, the timeline from the start of Phase I to final certification often ranges **10–12 weeks**, depending on the OSC's preparedness and whether remediation is needed. For executives, this means that achieving CMMC certification requires not only strong cybersecurity practices but also thoughtful planning and resource allocation. The CAP is not simply an audit—it is a disciplined, standardized process that demonstrates to the Department of War that a company is a trustworthy steward of sensitive defense information.

Why the CAP Matters

The CMMC Assessment Process (CAP) is essential because it sets the standard for how contractors are evaluated for compliance with cybersecurity requirements. It is more than a procedural step—it establishes a consistent way to assess whether an OSC meets both NIST SP 800-171 standards and broader CMMC requirements. The CAP's main goal is to ensure that assessments are consistent, no matter who performs them, and that high quality is maintained throughout. By enforcing a uniform process, the CAP upholds the integrity of CMMC assessments, building confidence among contractors, the Department of War, and the Defense Industrial Base.

For the DOW, the CAP ensures that contractors have more than just policies—they must have functional, effective safeguards. For executives, understanding the CAP is crucial, as certification affects contract eligibility, revenue, and reputation within the defense supply chain.

The Players: Roles and Responsibilities

The CAP defines clear roles for all involved in the assessment process. While cybersecurity professionals and auditors carry out technical evaluations, leadership involvement is critical for coordinating contracts, resources, and communication.

An OSC is a company seeking certification, and its executives, managers, and staff must provide documents, evidence, and system access. An Affirming

Official, typically a senior leader, is responsible for attesting to the accuracy and completeness of the information presented.

Assessments are conducted by C3PAOs—independent, accredited organizations—with teams of Certified Assessors (CCAs) led by a Lead CCA. Oversight bodies like The Cyber AB (a nonprofit designated by the DOW) manage accreditation and quality assurance. The Authorized Certifying Official in each C3PAO has the authority to issue certificates.

Checks and balances are fundamental to the CAP. No single person influences the outcome; impartiality, consistency, and quality assurance are built into the process to maintain trust across the defense community.

Preliminary Proceedings: Laying the Groundwork

Before formal assessment begins, several preparatory steps are essential. These administrative and contractual steps set the stage for the entire process.

The OSC first selects an accredited C3PAO from the official CMMC Marketplace, ensuring that the assessment is done by a qualified organization. The C3PAO verifies the OSC's legal entity with its CAGE code—a unique identifier from the DOW.

Both parties then agree on the assessment scope, determining which systems, facilities, and assets will be reviewed. A scope that is too narrow may overlook risks, while one that is too broad can make the assessment unnecessarily complex and expensive.

A conflict-of-interest review ensures assessor independence, confirming that assessors have not provided consulting services to the OSC. Once independence is verified, the relationship is formalized with a contract and a non-disclosure agreement.

For management, this stage is akin to preparing for a financial audit or major external review; careful planning here reduces surprises later in the process.

Phase I: Conduct the Pre-Assessment

The first formal phase of the CAP evaluates whether the OSC is ready for a full assessment. This is not about passing or failing security requirements, but about confirming readiness.

The C3PAO begins by reviewing the System Security Plan (SSP), the document that describes how the OSC addresses each of the required security controls. The review checks for completeness and consistency but does not yet judge effectiveness. The assessors also validate that the agreed-upon scope is accurate and that all relevant assets are included.

Another key activity is confirming that the OSC can provide evidence—policies, procedures, system logs, or staff interviews—to demonstrate how controls are implemented. If evidence is missing or unavailable, the OSC may not be ready to proceed.

At the end of this phase, the Lead Assessor makes a readiness determination. If the organization is not sufficiently prepared, the process is paused. Importantly, assessors cannot provide consulting advice on how to "fix" issues, as this would compromise their neutrality.

For executives, Phase I is a litmus test. It shows whether their organization has invested the time and resources necessary for a successful outcome. Failing readiness wastes time and money, while being well-prepared sets the stage for efficiency.

Phase 2: Assess Conformity to Security Requirements

Phase 2 is the heart of the CAP—the moment when assessors test whether cybersecurity practices are actually in place and effective.

The phase begins with an In-Brief Meeting, where assessors and company representatives align objectives, schedule, and roles. This meeting sets expectations and allows for clarification before testing begins.

The actual assessment involves the assessment team employing for each assessment objective a minimum or two of the three evaluation methods, as defined by NIST SP 800-171A: examine documents and records, interview personnel to confirm knowledge and responsibilities, and test systems or processes to see if controls are working.

Assessors use sampling techniques to balance depth and efficiency. They do not review every piece of evidence but instead focus on representative samples that provide confidence in overall compliance. If weaknesses are found, samples may be expanded.

An important element is the evaluation of external service providers (ESPs), such as Managed Service Providers (MSPs) or Cloud Service Providers (CSPs). If these providers handle CUI, they must themselves meet CMMC or FedRAMP standards.

Results from Phase 2 are converted into a score, reflecting whether each requirement is Met, Not Met, or Not Applicable. This score directly determines certification outcomes.

For executives, Phase 2 is where preparation pays off. Organizations that have integrated security into daily operations tend to provide strong, consistent evidence. Those that rely on last-minute document collection often struggle.

Phase 3: Complete and Report Assessment Results

By the time Phase 3 begins, all evidence collection is complete. The focus now shifts to documenting, reviewing, and reporting the results.

The assessment team compiles findings into a formal report. A separate quality assurance reviewer within the C3PAO verifies accuracy and ensures that the team followed CAP rules. This step prevents bias or inconsistency from influencing outcomes.

The results are then presented to the OSC during an Out-Brief Meeting. This meeting communicates the outcome but does not offer remediation guidance. If the OSC disagrees with the results, it may file an appeal first with the C3PAO and, if necessary, escalated to The Cyber AB.

For company leaders, this phase is about business impact. The findings determine whether the OSC will be eligible for contracts requiring CMMC certification. Even if some items are marked "Not Met," the possibility of a conditional certificate provides a path forward while remediation is completed.

Phase 4: Issue Certificate and Close Out POA&M

The final phase concludes the process with certification.

If all requirements are satisfied, the OSC receives a Final Certificate of CMMC Status. If some deficiencies remain but are formally tracked in a Plan of Action and Milestones (POA&M), a Conditional Certificate may be issued. This allows the OSC to compete for contracts while completing remediation.

Closing out a POA&M requires additional review by a C3PAO to verify that corrective actions were implemented. Once completed, the OSC receives its Final Certificate.

Certificates are delivered electronically to the OSC, The Cyber AB, and entered into the DOW's systems of record. They serve as official proof of compliance and are valid for a defined period.

For executives, this stage represents both achievement and accountability. Certification confirms that the organization meets DOW standards, but it also imposes responsibility to maintain those standards continuously.

Key Takeaways for Executives

The CAP is a structured, impartial process designed to protect national security while maintaining fairness in the defense supply chain. For executives, the key lessons are clear:

- CMMC is a requirement, not a choice. Without certification, contracts may be lost.
- Readiness matters. Preparation and documentation determine efficiency and success.
- Leadership involvement is essential. The CAP is not just a technical review; it is a business process that requires executive oversight.
- Certification is ongoing. Achieving it once is not enough—continuous monitoring and improvement are required.

Understanding CMMC Assessments

How invasive is a CMMC assessment?

Many people seem to think that during a CMMC assessment, the assessment teams will run rampant through the contractor's office, rummaging through filing cabinets and IT systems on the hunt for mishandled FCI or CUI. That simply is not the case.

The assessment is the validation that the contractor has properly implemented the appropriate requirements for their CMMC level. It focuses more on the structure of the program and ensuring that the organization's business practices are being followed. It is not a detailed audit that inspects every minute detail.

An assessment can take as few as 2 and as many as five or more days. The following is an example of how a Lead Certified CMMC Assessor (CCA) and assessment team might structure a five-day Level 2 assessment for an SMB environment handling CUI.

It assumes:

- ✅ One or two physical sites,
- ✅ ~1 week total assessment time,
- ✅ On-site + virtual hybrid approach.

Day	Activities
Monday (Day 1)	✅ On-site kickoff meeting (In-Brief). ✅ Physical walkthrough of in-scope facilities (server rooms, labs, CUI storage areas, badge systems, visitor controls). ✅ Begin interviews with key personnel onsite. ✅ Set up remote working logistics (FedRAMP Moderate virtual meeting/evidence sharing).
Tuesday (Day 2)	✅ Continue interviews (IT, engineering, HR, compliance, management). ✅ Review documentation (policies, procedures). ✅ Examine technical configurations (access controls, MFA, logging, network security).
Wednesday (Day 3)	✅ Conduct technical verification (live screen shares, system demos). ✅ Review operational evidence (incident response records, training logs, patching history).

	✅ Follow-up on any unclear findings.
Wednesday (Day 3)	✅ Finalize deep-dive reviews. ✅ Resolve open questions. ✅ Hold internal assessment team QA checkpoint to prepare preliminary results.
Wednesday (Day 3)	✅ Present formal Out-Brief to OSC leadership (virtual or on-site). ✅ Walk through preliminary assessment results, including MET/NOT MET summary and potential POA&M items. ✅ Provide next steps overview.

How long is a CMMC assessment?

From the OSC's perspective, the active portion of most CMMC assessments take place over the course of a single week. The assessment team will need to speak with your people and, in many cases, tour your facilities. However, if your compliance program is well-structured, properly documented, and does not require a site visit, the active portion of the assessment may be completed in less time. Much of that time will be spent with the assessment team members asking your team about documentation you provided or to demonstrate a process.

What components of my company are assessed?

CMMC focuses on identifying the sensitive information handled by a contractor, and then ensuring that the **assets** (i.e., the locations, people, technology, and processes) that handle, or manage the handling of, the information will properly safeguard the information. The collection of these assets is referred to as the assessment "**scope**".

At CMMC Level 1, only the assets that handle FCI are in scope. If the asset does not store, process, or transmit FCI, it does not need to be assessed.

At CMMC Level 2, things get more complicated. The CMMC Scoping Guide Level 2 defines six categories of assets: CUI Assets, Security Protection Assets, Contractor Risk Managed Assets, Specialized Assets, and Out-of-Scope Assets.

CUI Assets - Assets that process, store, or transmit CUI. CUI Assets must be assessed against all of the requirements in NIST SP 800-171.

Security Protection Assets (SPA) - Assets that provide security functions or capabilities to the environment being assessed. Each SPA must be assessed against the NIST SP 800-171 requirements that are relevant to the capabilities provided by the SPA.

Contractor Risk Managed Assets (CRMA) - Assets that, because of the way an organization's building is constructed or network is architected, are not physically or logically separated from CUI Assets but which are not intended to handle CUI because of the organization's security-related business processes. CRMAs must be listed in the organization's **System Security Plan (SSP)**, and the SSP must also describe how the asset is secured or otherwise treated to mitigate risk. If sufficiently documented, CRMAs are not assessed against the NIST SP 800-171 requirements. However, if the contractor's risk-based security practices or other findings raise questions about the assets, assessors can conduct a limited check to identify deficiencies. In the end, contractors should limit the use of CRMAs and ensure that alternative, compensating mechanisms are in place to protect the CRMAs.

Specialized Assets – Assets, such as **Internet of Things (IoT)** devices, **Industrial Internet of Things (IIoT)** devices, **Operational Technology (OT)**, **Government Furnished Equipment (GFE)**, **Restricted Information Systems**, and **Test Equipment**, that can process, store, or transmit CUI but are unable to be fully secured. Specialized assets must be documented in the asset inventory and the SSP must show how the assets are managed using the organization's security practices. Assessors must review the treatment of Specialized Assets in the SSP, but the Specialized Assets are not assessed against other NIST SP 800-171 requirements.

Out-of-Scope Assets – Assets that cannot process, store, or transmit CUI; do not provide security protections for CUI assets; and which are physically or logically separated from CUI Assets. The organization should be prepared to justify how the physical or logical separation prevents the Out-of-Scope Assets from storing, processing, or transmitting CUI.

How does this change at CMMC Level 3?

At CMMC Level 3, CRMAs are treated as CUI Assets and are assessed against all of the CMMC Level 2 and CMMC Level 3 security requirements. SPAs are assessed against all of the CMMC Level 2 and CMMC Level 3 requirements that are relevant to the capabilities provided by the SPA. Specialized Assets are assessed against all CMMC Level 2 and CMMC Level 3 security requirements.

What did you mean when you mentioned "locations, people, technology, and processes"?

As previously discussed, the CMMC program is designed to ensure that the government's sensitive information is properly safeguarded. This includes both electronic and physical copies of that information.

To do this effectively, an organization needs to understand the organization's assets that handle the sensitive information. These assets generally fall into four categories: Locations, People, Technology, and Processes.

Locations – These are the physical or electronic locations at which the sensitive information is stored, processed, or transmitted. This includes, for example, the office building where paper copies of sensitive information are stored, a server closet that holds computer equipment used to process sensitive information, and cloud services used to store or process sensitive information. Creating an inventory of the locations where sensitive information is handled allows the organization to ensure that proper safeguards are in place.

People – These are the people who are authorized to access sensitive information. It is important to remember that access to CUI must be restricted to only those persons with a lawful government purpose to access that CUI. Although FCI has a little more flexibility, as a practical matter only those whose job requires them to access the FCI should be granted access. Creating an inventory of the people with access to sensitive information helps the organization ensure that access is properly limited and that the individuals are appropriately trained in the safeguarding of sensitive information.

Technology – These are the systems, tools, and services used to handle or secure sensitive information. These may include, for example, an organization's E-mail system, ERP system, offsite backup provider, endpoint detection and response tools, software development environments, and end-user desktop or laptop devices. Creating an inventory of these technologies helps the organization ensure that it limits access to sensitive information to only the tools, services, and systems authorized to access that information.

Processes – These are the business processes that define how the organization secures and handles sensitive information. Business processes are typically written policies and corresponding procedures and plans. Creating an inventory of the organization's existing business processes helps the organization ensure that its processes align with the corresponding CMMC security requirements.

What is the difference between a CMMC Level 2 Self-Assessment and a CMMC Level 2 Certification Assessment?

Contractors who handle CUI must ensure that they are meeting all of the requirements specified in NIST SP 800-171 Rev. 2,, as further refined in NIST SP 800-171A. To do this, all contractors are required to conduct a **CMMC Level 2 Self-Assessment**. The contractor must then submit an affirmation of compliance to DOW.

As previously noted, DOW estimates that about ninety-five percent (95%) of contractors who handle CUI will also need a **CMMC Level 2 Certification Assessment**. This is conducted by an independent C3PAO and validates the contractor's affirmation of compliance. Upon successful validation, the C3PAO issues a certification of compliance to the contractor. This independent validation, and the corresponding certification, increase DOW's trust in the contractor's ability to handle CUI.

Contracts that require only a self-assessment are those that involve CUI that is not listed in the Defense Organizational Index Grouping. These types of CUI are important but don't pose high risks to national security if exposed Examples includes routine administrative data, standard operating procedures, and basic acquisition or logistics information.

Contracts that will require third party certification are those that involve CUI that is listed in the Defense Organizational Index Grouping on the CUI Registry. This includes more sensitive categories, such as: Defense-critical technologies (e.g., weapons specs, UAV systems), Military planning or operations data, Export-controlled technical data (like ITAR or EAR info), and nuclear or space-related design information.

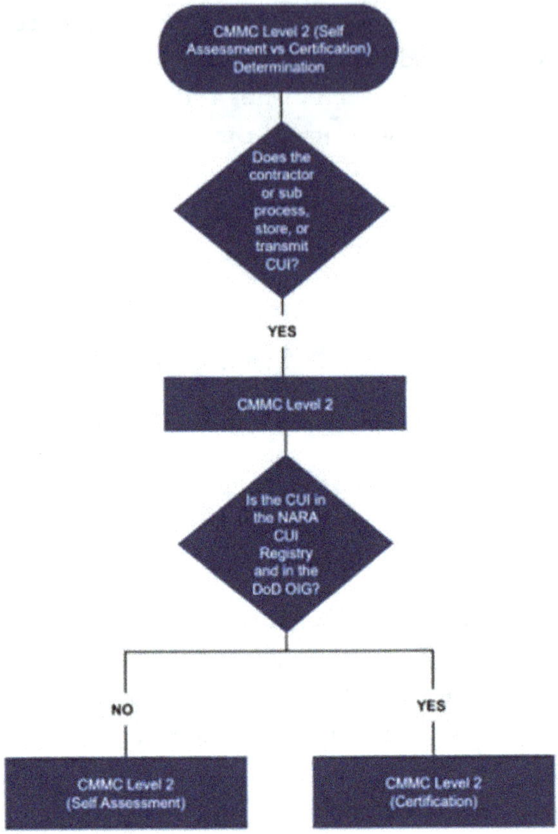

Figure 8

What is the difference between a CMMC Level 2 Certification Assessment and a CMMC Level 3 Certification Assessment?

Certain prime contractors (DOW currently estimates it to be less than 1% of all DOW contractors) who work on DOW's critical programs will need to demonstrate that their information security programs meet additional security requirements on top of those in NIST SP 800-171. These additional safeguarding requirements come from NIST SP 800-

172. DOW has indicated that contractors will need to implement 24 of

the NIST SP 800-172 requirements as defined in Table 1 to 32 CFR 170.14(c)(4). These requirements are: 3.1.2e, 3.1.3e, 3.2.1e, 3.2.2e, 3.4.1e, 3.4.2e, 3.4.3e, 3.5.1e, 3.5.3e, 3.6.1e, 3.6.2e, 3.9.2e, 3.11.1e, 3.11.2e, 3.11.3e, 3.11.4e, 3.11.5e, 3.11.6e, 3.11.7e, 3.12.1e, 3.13.4e, 3.14.1e, 3.14.3e, and 3.14.6e.

Contractors who see CMMC Level 3 Certification Assessment requirements in their contracts must first obtain a CMMC Level 2 Certification Assessment for the covered contractor information system from a C3PAO. Then the contractor coordinates with DIBCAC who will conduct the assessment of the 24 additional requirements in NIST SP 800-172 for that covered contractor information system. If the contractor passes the assessment, the contractor will be awarded a certificate of compliance from DIBCAC.

Will Assessors need access to CUI?

Although CMMC assessors will observe how your employees interact with the environment and systems that handle FCI and CUI, the assessors should essentially never need to handle or have access to any CUI or FCI.

During the assessment, the assessors may inadvertently observe FCI or CUI as your team demonstrates how certain processes are performed.

As an example of this, imagine that the door to a room that holds CUI is supposed to be locked. However, when your team member attempts to demonstrate that the door is locked, their badge accidentally swipes against the badge reader and unlocks the door, allowing your team member to open it. When the door opens, the assessor is able to observe some of the information in the room.

Another example is where your team is sharing their screen so an assessor can verify the configuration of certain software. When your team member closes the configuration screen, a document containing CUI is momentarily visible to the assessor.

These inadvertent disclosures are unlikely to happen but may still occur. At the same time, your team should be thoughtful about any requests made by the assessors and report any suspected attempts by the assessor to directly access FCI or CUI.

What should I have ready when I contact the C3PAO for my CMMC assessment?

The C3PAO will expect you to have the following information available:

Network Diagram

- illustrates the basic network architecture of the in-scope assets and clearly defines the boundary

Data Inventory/Data Flow Diagram

- identifies how FCI and/or CUI information is received by the system, how it moves through the organization, and how it leaves

System Security Plan

- includes a description of how your organization meets each Assessment Objective in NIST SP 800-171

Evidence

- a set of adequate and sufficient evidence that demonstrates to the assessment team that the organization is performing the activities described in your SSP. This can include written policies, procedures, plans, screen captures, lists, and other documentation.

What should I expect during a CMMC C3PAO assessment?

The process begins with the contractor interviewing one or more C3PAOs. The goal of the interview is to find someone who is familiar with the overall structure of the contractor's business and the types of technologies used by the contractor. For example, if the contractor is a manufacturing business, the contractor might want to select a C3PAO who is familiar with CNC and other equipment and the issues involved with maintaining such equipment.

Once a C3PAO is selected, the contractor will give the C3PAO access to, or copies of, the contractor's SSP and related documents at least 10 business days prior to the assessment. The Lead Assessor will review those documents to ensure that there is adequate and sufficient evidence to proceed with the assessment.

The next step is for the assessment team to review the documentation in detail, requesting additional information if necessary. During the formal assessment, the Assessment Team will conduct interviews, observe testing of your business processes, and conduct any necessary site visits.

Throughout the assessment process, the Assessment Team will provide the contractor with status updates. This includes "trending" reports at the end of each day during the "live" portion of the assessment. These trending reports indicate the status of the NIST SP 800-171 requirements that have been reviewed, including any that may be "trending not met". The C3PAO may also allow the contractor to correct minor deficiencies during the assessment.

What is the difference between Conditional and Final status?

FAR 52.204-21 and NIST SP 800-171 are designed for flexibility. They have been written as a set of required outcomes, rather than a set of implementation-specific requirements. This flexibility allows contractors and others who are implementing information security programs to tailor their approach to match the way their organization conducts business.

Under CMMC, if the organization's information security program meets the requirements for their appropriate CMMC level, the organization will earn a "**Final**" status. For example in CMMC Level 2, if a C3PAO's assessment team agrees that the contractor's information security program meets the requirements in NIST SP 800-171, the contractor will earn a "**Final Level 2 (C3PAO)**" status and the C3PAO will also issue the contractor a certification. Similarly, for those contractors handling CUI who can self-assess, if their internal assessment finds that their information security program meets the requirements in NIST SP 800-171, the organization will deem itself to have earned a status of "**Final Level 2 (Self)**".

NIST SP 800-171's flexibility can sometimes lead to disagreements between those implementing the requirements and those assessing the implementation as to whether the implementation meets the NIST SP 800-171 requirements and all of the corresponding NIST SP 800-171A Assessment Objectives. This means that, during an assessment, a contractor may learn that certain aspects of their information security program do not meet the NIST SP 800-171 requirements. The contractor must document these "not met" requirements, along with a plan to fix or "remediate" them, in a Close-out **Plan of Action & Milestone (POA&M)**.

DOW has introduced the concept of a "**Conditional**" status in CMMC Levels 2 and 3 to give contractors 180 days to remediate the POA&Ms that resulted from their assessment (referred to as a **POA&M Closeout Period**). Without this Conditional status, the contractor could have been subject to immediate termination of their contract, they may have faced other contractual remedies, and there could have been other consequences as well.

What Limitations are there on Conditional status?

It is important to note that Conditional status is not available under CMMC Level 1. All requirements must be met in full at the time the contractor submits their self-assessment results to DOW.

Conditional status is only available in CMMC Level 2 under certain conditions. These include:

- Using the scoring outlined in 32 CFR 170.24(c)(2)(i)(B), the contractor's score is at least 80% (i.e., >=88) of the possible Level 2 score;

- None of the requirements addressed by a POA&M have a point value of greater than 1 except SC.L2-3.13.11 CUI Encryption, which may be included on a POA&M if encryption is employed but it is not FIPS-validated, which would result in a point value of 3; and,
- None of the following security requirements are addressed by any POA&M:
  - AC.L2-3.1.20 External Connections (CUI Data).
  - AC.L2-3.1.22 Control Public Information (CUI Data).
  - CA.L2-3.12.4 System Security Plan.
  - PE.L2-3.10.3 Escort Visitors (CUI Data).
  - PE.L2-3.10.4 Physical Access Logs (CUI Data).
  - PE.L2-3.10.5 Manage Physical Access (CUI Data).

For CMMC Level 3, conditional status is only available under certain conditions. These include:

- Using the scoring outlined in 32 CFR 170.24(c)(3), the contractor's score is at least 80% (i.e., >=20) of the possible Level 3 score; and,
- None of following security requirements are addressed by a POA&M:
  - IR.L3-3.6.1e Security Operations Center.
  - IR.L3-3.6.2e Cyber Incident Response Team.
  - RA.L3-3.11.1e Threat-Informed Risk Assessment.
  - RA.L3-3.11.6e Supply Chain Risk Response.
  - RA.L3-3.11.7e Supply Chain Risk Plan.
  - RA.L3-3.11.4e Security Solution Rationale.
  - SI.L3-3.14.3e Specialized Asset Security.

What are Operational Plans of Action, and How are they Different from POA&Ms?

As discussed in the previous answer, NIST SP 800-171 is designed to give contractors flexibility in the way they design and operate their information security programs. This includes, for example, requirements 3.11.2, 3.11.3, 3.12.2, and 3.13.2. When read together, these require and allow the contractor to:

- perform periodic vulnerability scans to identify known weaknesses in the contractor's information systems;
- remediate identified vulnerabilities in accordance with risk assessments;
- develop plans of action to correct deficiencies and reduce or eliminate vulnerabilities in the contractor's information systems; and
- employ system engineering principles that promote effective information security.

Put more simply, these requirements allow a contractor to deviate from a fully compliant state when the risks of remaining compliant outweigh the risks associated with the deviation. These deviations are referred to as "**Temporary Deficiencies**" in CMMC 2.13. It is important to note that a Temporary Deficiency is not based on an 'in progress' initial implementation of a CMMC security requirement; instead, they arise after implementation.

The contractor is expected to track these Temporary Deficiencies in "**Operational Plans of Action**". The Operational Plans of Action help the contractor ensure that their information security program is brought back into compliance as soon as practicable.

As a practical example of how Operational Plans of Action can be used, requirement 3.13.11[b] necessitate the use of FIPS-validated cryptographic modules when encrypting. However, vendors occasionally publish patches to their cryptographic modules that fix vulnerabilities that are actively being exploited, but those patches have not undergone the FIPS validation process. From a risk management perspective, the risk to the organization of not applying the patch is likely to be significantly higher than the risk to the organization that the patch will not properly implement encryption. Therefore, the organization would apply the patch but track the deviation as an Operational Plan of Action. The contractor should periodically review their Operational Plans of Action so that any available updates (e.g., newer, FIPS-validated versions of the cryptographic module) can be applied in a timely manner.

What are Enduring Exceptions?

Enduring Exceptions are special circumstances or systems where remediation and full compliance with CMMC security requirements is not feasible. Examples include systems required to replicate the configuration of 'fielded' systems, medical devices, test equipment, OT, IoT, Specialized Assets, and Government Furnished Equipment. No operational plan of action is required but the circumstance and any remediation must be documented within the contractor's system security plan. All properly documented Enduring Exceptions are assessed as Met.

Enhancing DOW Supply Chain Visibility

Why does the US government need contracts?

The United States Government purchases goods and services from a vast number of organizations around the world. The government uses contracts as a mechanism for defining the nature, quantity, price, and other details about those goods and services. Those supplying goods and services to the government are part of its "**supply chain**".

Why is the US government suddenly adding information security requirements to its contracts?

It isn't. At the Executive Branch level, the government has had requirements for securing unclassified information in its contracts since at least 2015. DOW has had requirements for securing unclassified information in its contracts since at least 2011.

As we saw during the 2020 global pandemic, issues in any one organization's supply chain can create effects that ripple across the entire nation. When those issues occur to the federal government, they can even place our national security at risk.

Almost every organization across the United States, including those in DOW's supply chain, use Internet-connected devices to help run their businesses. Among other tasks, these devices handle DOW's sensitive, unclassified information.

This is information which, if it fell into the wrong hands, could have a significant impact on US citizens, members of the US military, and our way of life. There are often laws, regulations, and other policies that require this information to be safeguarded when it is entrusted to or created by/on behalf of the government. When that information is stolen or released without authorization, it can create significant issues for the government and the nation.

DOW now is seeking assurances that its contractors' Internet-connected devices are properly configured to safeguard DOW's sensitive information. Their goal is to help reduce the likelihood of an incident that has long-term impacts on the nation.

What is the difference between a prime contractor and a subcontractor?

When the United States Government purchases goods or services from those in its supply chain, it always does so with a single entity: the "**prime contractor**." May prime contractors cannot fulfill all of the contract's requirements themselves. Instead, they enter into contracts with others (**subcontractors**) to fulfill portions of the government contract's requirements.

Why are prime contractors so concerned about their subcontractors' performance?

As previously noted, the government enters into a contract with only one entity, the prime contractor. Due to a legal concept referred to as "**privity of contract**", the government cannot generally reach through to a subcontractor to work directly with them or hold them accountable for their performance under the contract. Instead, the prime contractor is accountable for almost everything done under the contract, including the subcontractors' performance. This creates a lot of risk for prime contractors.

As a result, many prime contractors are careful to ensure that their contracts with their subcontractors a) "**flow down**" (i.e., pass along or include) all of the requirements from the contract with the government, and b) give the prime contractors leverage if the subcontractor makes a material misstep. Prime contractors also often include tools for validating that their subcontractors are meeting those contractual requirements before and during the contractors and hold the subcontractors accountable when they are not in compliance.

Where can I find the typical requirements in government contracts?

Writing contracts is tricky. To streamline that process and standardize the requirements across the millions of contracts that it enters into each year, the government created a set of pre-written contract provisions and clauses. These can be found in the Federal Acquisition Regulations (FAR).

Can agencies create their own contractual requirements?

Yes. While the FAR provides a high-level acquisition framework, many agencies need to tailor the requirements, or add other requirements, because of the agencies' unique attributes. For DOW, these requirements are published in the Defense Federal Acquisition Regulations Supplement (DFARS).

What are mandatory contract clauses?

As they write **Requests for Information** (**RFIs**), **Requests for Proposals** (**RFPs**), and the resulting contracts, DOW's Contracting Officers select the appropriate clauses from the FAR and DFARS based on the nature of the work being performed under the contract. In some cases, the government has identified the requirements in certain clauses to be so important that they must be incorporated into all contracts. These mandatory clauses address various factors, such as payment terms.

What are the mandatory flow down clauses?

In some cases, contract requirements are so important to the government that they require prime contractors to always flow down the requirements to all subcontractors. This means the prime contractors must ensure that any contract between the prime contractor and their subcontractors contains these mandatory requirements, and the contract must also direct subcontractors to flow down the requirements to their subcontractors as well. These clauses include, for example, FAR 52.204-21, which covers the basic safeguarding requirements for **Federal Contract Information** (**FCI**).

In certain, limited cases, although the clauses are generally required, the government allows the prime contractor to not flow down the clause when specific conditions are met. For example DFARS 252.204-7012 need not be flowed down to a subcontractor when the contract does not involve **Covered Defense Information** (**CDI**) or other **Controlled Unclassified Information** (**CUI**).

What impact can noncompliance have on a contractor?

Failure to comply with contractual requirements, regardless of whether the noncompliance is by the prime contractor or a subcontractor, puts the prime contractor in breach of the contract with the government. This can result in significant consequences for the prime contractor, including fines and penalties, termination of contracts, non-renewal of existing contracts, and debarment.

What is DOW doing to encourage/require compliance?

DOW is pushing its supply chain to comply with all aspects of contracts, with particular attention to cybersecurity. One motivation for this is that DOW faces its own legal obligations associated with the handling of the government's non-public, unclassified information (i.e., FCI and CUI). In this book, FCI and CUI are referred to collectively as the government's "**sensitive information**".

DOW needs to ensure that its contractors can properly protect sensitive information when that sensitive information is created by the contractors or received by the contractors from the government, otherwise the failure to properly protect the sensitive information can create legal issues for DOW.

Another motivation is to protect our warfighters. Many contractors are handling information that is valuable to our adversaries. When contractors do not protect sensitive information appropriately, our adversaries can easily steal the information. This allows the adversaries to more easily target our warfighters and compete with them on the battlefield, making conflicts last longer and more deadly.

Given these and other pressures, DOW introduced two major cybersecurity initiatives over the past few years. One of them is a short-term fix, and the other is a much larger program.

The short-term initiative is embodied in the clauses at DFARS 252.204-7019 and DFARS 252.204-7020. The -7019 clause requires all contractors who handle CUI to self-assess their compliance with certain cybersecurity requirements and to report a resulting score to the Supplier Performance Risk System (**SPRS**). The score, which can range from -203 to 110, is calculated based on the requirements that have yet to be implemented by the contractor. That is, you start with 110 points and lose 5, 3, or 1 point for each applicable requirement that is not fully met. DOW's goal is for all contractors who handle CUI to achieve (honest) 110-point scores in SPRS.

As a mechanism for addressing the potential fraud that goes along with self-assessments and reporting, DOW also introduced the -7020 clause. The -7020 clause allows DOW to audit any contractor, including subcontractors, to confirm that the contractor's stated score is accurate. As you can probably imagine, the -7020 clause must be flowed down by prime contractors to their subcontractors.

The longer-term initiative is the Cybersecurity Maturity Model Certification (**CMMC**) program. Under CMMC, all DOW contractors will be required to perform self-assessments of their cybersecurity program against the requirements in either FAR 52.204-12 (if they are only handling FCI), NIST SP 800-171 Rev. 2 (if they are handling CUI), or NIST SP 800-171 Rev. 2 + portions of NIST SP 800-172 (if they are a prime contractor working on a critical program). A senior level Affirming Official must submit an annual affirmation that the company complies with the appropriate requirements.

In addition, DOW will soon require all contractors who handle CUI, with limited exceptions, to obtain a CMMC certification issued by an authorized third party, referred to as a **CMMC 3rd Party Assessment Organization (C3PAO)**. This certification validates the contractor's compliance with the requirements in NIST SP 800-171 Rev. 2 and that the contractor can properly safeguard the government's information.

Prime contractors working on critical DOW programs will need not only a certification of their compliance with NIST SP 800-171 Rev. 2, but also a separate certification, issued by DIBCAC. This additional certification validates the contractor's compliance with twenty-four (24) of the requirements in NIST SP 800-172. These are designed to ensure prime contractors are prepared to address attacks by nation states and other highly sophisticated attackers (referred to as **Advanced Persistent Threats (APTs)**).

All required CMMC affirmations and certifications must be in place before the contract is awarded or the award may be rescinded and the contract awarded to someone else. DOW's Contracting Officers will confirm that these affirmations and the corresponding certifications are in place by reviewing information in SPRS.

How much trouble can a contractor face if they have not implemented the security requirements by the necessary time?

Over the past four administrations, the United States Government has taken progressively stronger stances which demonstrate the important role information security and cybersecurity play in the country's national security. As part of that process, in October of 2021 the United States Department of Justice (**DOJ**) announced its "Civil Cyber Fraud Initiative" in which it began more aggressively identifying and pursuing contractors who are not meeting the cybersecurity and information security protection requirements defined in their government contracts.

Although the Civil Cyber Fraud Initiative is still in its infancy, it is already yielding results, including several multi-million-dollar settlements.

Contractors should also be aware that, under the False Claims Act, the government can fine contractors up to 3x the value of the corresponding contract **PLUS** $11,000+ per "claim" for misrepresenting the contractor's compliance with material contractual provisions like the cybersecurity and information security clauses. Contractors can even face other actions, including being "**debarred**" (prohibited from participating in future contracts) and the termination of existing contracts.

How can DOW or DoJ catch noncompliant contractors?

There are several ways, including when:

- the contractor is the victim of a cyber incident, and the perpetrators publish information about the contractor and their deficiencies online (e.g., after the contractor refuses to pay a ransom);
- the contractor is a victim of a cyber incident and reports the incident to DOW who, while performing an audit to determine the scope of any damage, identifies material deficiencies;
- the contractor's own actions make it clear to DOW that certain requirements are not met (e.g., the contractor sends unencrypted/improperly encrypted CUI via E-mail to a DOW employee); or

- an employee of the contractor reports the contractor's noncompliance to DOW (i.e., they are a "**whistleblower"**) or takes up the case on their own.

What are whistleblowers?

In this context, whistleblowers are people with inside knowledge of a government contractor's noncompliance. Whistleblowers must attempt to get the contractor to resolve the noncompliance first but, if that does not happen, the whistleblower can report the noncompliance to the government. They can even bring a lawsuit on behalf of the government.

Whistleblowers can receive up to **25-33% of any financial settlement** or court-awarded damages that arise from the reported case. These strong financial incentives, coupled with increasing awareness of compliance requirements, have resulted in a significant increase in the number of whistleblower cases.

We don't handle CUI; why is our prime asking us to submit a score to SPRS?

When a contract is awarded, the prime contractor attests to the fact that all contractors handling CUI on the contract have submitted scores to SPRS. Since there is a lot of confusion about what constitutes CUI, many prime contractors simply assume that all their subcontractors will handle CUI. They are therefore requiring all subcontractors to perform self-assessments and record scores in SPRS.

What information is collected in SPRS?

When you submit your score to SPRS, the government only asks for some basic information, such as your company name, Commercial and Government Entity (**CAGE**) code, and score. The government does not want to be a repository for contractors' System Security Plans (**SSP**), Plans of Action and Milestones (**POA&M**), or other security-related information.

What is SPRS?

SPRS (typically pronounced "spurz") is a web-enabled enterprise application accessed through the Procurement Integrated Enterprise Environment (PIEE). SPRS gathers, processes, and displays data about the performance of suppliers. SPRS is DOW's single, authorized application to retrieve suppliers' performance information.

SPRS alerts procurement specialists to **Federal Supply Classification/ Product Service Code (FSC/PSC)** specific risks and risk mitigations. SPRS's **Supplier Risk Score** provides procurement specialists with a composite score that considers each supplier's performance in the areas of product delivery and quality. The quality and delivery classifications identified for a supplier in SPRS may be used by the contracting officer to evaluate a supplier's performance.

SPRS provides storage and retrieval for the NIST SP 800-171 assessment results and maintains the National Security Systems (NSS) Restricted List.

Suppliers/Vendors may view their own company information in SPRS.

What do I need to access SPRS?

To access SPRS, you will need to create an account in PIEE. The process for creating a PIEE account can be found here: https://piee.eb.mil/xhtml/unauth/web/homepage/vendorGettingStartedHelp.xhtml

What information can prime contractors ask for?

As commercial entities, the prime contractors can largely set whatever requirements they like for determining who should qualify as a subcontractor. They can, therefore, ask for a lot of information, including your current SPRS score, your SSP, and your POA&Ms.

Must I give a prime contractor everything they ask for?

Not necessarily. As a practical matter, you can always push back and ask why they need the information, how it will be protected, etc. before you share it with them. However, the prime contractor can also choose not to do business with your company.

One way to help mitigate some of the risk is through a platform like FutureFeed. You can give specific individuals in the prime contractor's company access to the information they need for a limited time, allowing them to gain their desired level of confidence while still allowing you to control your information.

Why are prime contractors pushing their subcontractors to earn higher scores for SPRS?

Back in 2020, DOW knew that it needed to make some changes to the way it evaluates proposals. DOW recognized that its traditional "lowest cost, technically acceptable" acquisition approach, and even some versions of the "best value" approach, created an inequity.

Under these traditional acquisition approaches, contracts were typically awarded with lowest cost as at least a leading, if not the primary, decision-making factor. However, contractors who did the right thing by implementing the required security programs faced higher operating costs. As a result, these same contractors were essentially penalized because they did the right thing since their costs were higher than their competitors. DOW created DFARS 252.204-7024, also referred to as "the -7024 clause", to help address this inequity.

The -7024 clause allows Contracting Officers to take information in SPRS, as well as other supply chain security information, into account when making an award. This allows the Contracting Officer to award contracts to those contractors, and contractor teams, who are taking the right steps to protect CUI. This is true even when the price of their goods or services is (within reason) higher than their competitors.

Prime Contractors want to know the score their subcontractors have recorded in SPRS so they can better assess their chances of successfully winning a proposal.

Federal Contract and Controlled Unclassified Information

What is Federal Contract Information (FCI)?

The **Federal Acquisition Regulations** (**FAR**) define **Federal Contract Information** (**FCI**) as "...information, not intended for public release, that is provided by or generated for the Government under a contract to develop or deliver a product or service to the Government, but not including information provided by the Government to the public (such as on public websites) or simple transactional information, such as necessary to process payments." [FAR 52.204-21(a)]

What are some examples of FCI?

Almost everything you create or receive under a government contract is FCI. This includes early drafts of deliverables and even E-mails with government employees.

What is Controlled Unclassified Information?

The CUI Program defines CUI as "...information the Government creates or possesses, or that an entity creates or possesses for or on behalf of the Government, that a law, regulation, or Government-wide policy requires or permits an agency to handle using safeguarding or dissemination controls. However, CUI does not include classified information ... or information a non-executive branch entity possesses and maintains in its own systems that did not come from, or was not created or possessed by or for, an executive branch agency or an entity acting for an agency." [32 CFR 2002.04(h)]

What are some examples of CUI?

Over 400 LRGWPs are formally authorized to serve as the basis for designating information as CUI. They cover a wide range of the government's information, including:

- law enforcement investigations and court proceedings;
- personnel records, student records, and genetic information;
- naval nuclear propulsion information; and
- information about corporate mergers, net worth, and retirement accounts.

Even E-mails can rise to the level of CUI depending on their content.

What is the difference between CUI Basic and CUI Specified?

Information is "**CUI Specified**" if the applicable LRGWP says the information can or must be safeguarded in a particular way, or that the information is subject to limited dissemination controls. For example, information that is subject to the International Traffic in Arms Regulations (**ITAR**) is CUI Specified because ITAR prohibits the dissemination of that information outside the United States, including to non-US persons, without a license.

If the LRGWP does not specify safeguarding or limited dissemination controls, then the information is "**CUI Basic**".

How do I know if something is CUI?

In most cases, information will be conspicuously marked with either "CUI" or "Controlled" in the header of the document (see Figure 9, below for an example) or on the media containing the information if the information is CUI.

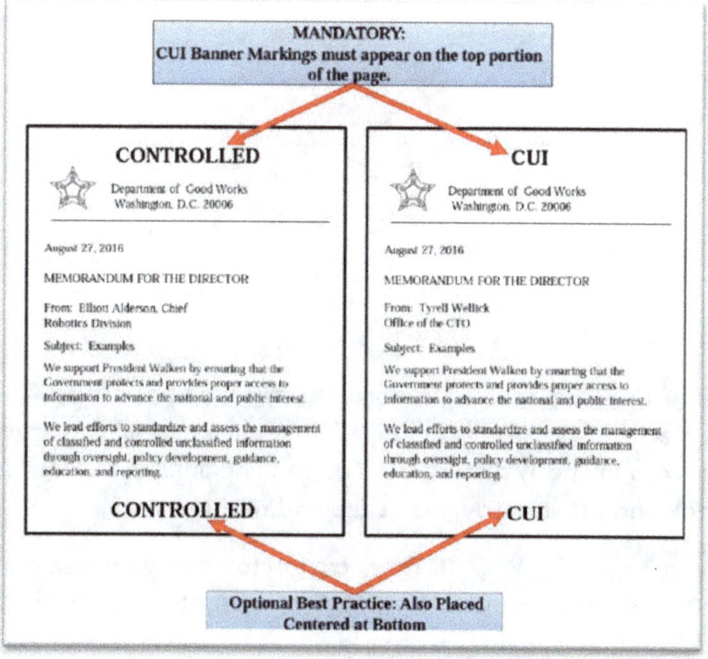

Figure 9

In some cases, such as where it is not possible to directly mark the information, it may be indirectly "marked" as CUI via language in a contract, appendix, memorandum, separate agreement, or other document.

As illustrated in Figure 10, below, in other cases, the computer system, container, or room in which the information is stored may be marked, rather than the information itself

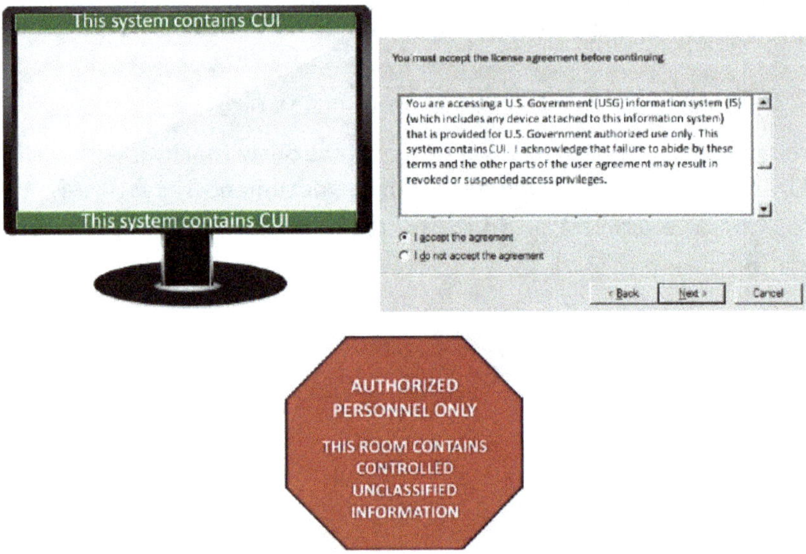

Figure 10

The **National Archives and Records Administration** (**NARA**) has published a CUI Marking Handbook that contains useful information about how to properly mark CUI. You can find links to the CUI Marking Handbook and other resources at the end of this book.

As a **Department of War** (**DOW**) contractor, you should be on the lookout for information marked with DOW Distribution Statements B-F. Figure 11, below, provides a sample distribution statement. CUI includes, by definition, information that is subject to dissemination controls. Therefore, if you find any information with distribution statements B-F, you should treat that information as CUI even if it is not explicitly marked with CUI markings.

Anatomy of a Distribution Statement

1. Authorized Audience or Who Can Access
2. Reason for Control or Why/Reason
3. Date of Determination
4. Controlling Office or Releasing Authority

Figure 11

How will I know if the information I create is CUI?

Your contract with the government will tell you, usually in the form of an attachment such as a **Security Classification Guide (SCG)**. In fact, the contract should not only tell you specifically which information you create is CUI, but it should also tell you how to mark the information, including an appropriate "**designation indicator**," and the corresponding LRGWP(s) that are the basis for designating the information CUI. If you do not have this information, you should ask for it. For more information on designation indicators, see the CUI Marking Handbook.

DOW contractors should note that, as discussed above, if their contract requires them to create information and mark that information with one or more of DOW's Distribution Statements B-F, that information has been designated as CUI and should be handled as such. You should ask your Contracting Officer for appropriate CUI markings if they have not been provided.

Is all legacy information (e.g., FOUO) automatically CUI?

No. Under the CUI program, the agency which created or owns the information must determine whether any information that contains legacy markings, such as **Sensitive but Unclassified (SBU)**, **For Official Use Only (FOUO)**, **Law Enforcement Sensitive (LES)**, etc., is CUI.

If an agency determines that legacy information is CUI, the agency must mark it appropriately before disseminating the information outside the agency. If the legacy information is in a contractor's possession, the agency must tell the contractor how to properly mark the information, and the contractor should ask the agency for the LRGWP that is the basis for the CUI designation. If the information is CUI Specified, then the information and anyone handling it is subject to additional safeguarding obligations. The only way for a contractor to be certain they are meeting those extra obligations is by knowing exactly which LRGWP applies.

To whom can CUI be disseminated?

Only persons with a Lawful Government Purpose are authorized to access (including receive) CUI. **Lawful Government Purpose** is defined as "any activity, mission, function, operation, or endeavor that the U.S. Government authorizes or recognizes within the scope of its legal authorities or the legal authorities of non-executive branch entities (such as state and local law enforcement)." [32 CFR 2002.04(bb)]

Although Lawful Government Purpose is a much broader standard than the "need-to-know" standard used for classified information, it is critical that contractors ensure that they only disseminate CUI to (and allow CUI to be accessed by) appropriate persons whose access will further the purpose of the corresponding contract. For example, the cleaning crew in an office most likely does not have a Lawful Government Purpose to access most CUI, and therefore steps should be taken to keep the cleaners from accessing CUI in the contractor's environment.

Where can I learn more about CUI?

NARA oversees the CUI program and maintains the authoritative list of all the LRGWPs that can be the basis for a CUI designation. This list is referred to as the "CUI Registry," and is a useful resource for contractors to better understand the different categories of information that an agency can designate as CUI.

In addition, NARA and DOW both offer free online CUI training. This training covers how to mark information as CUI once an agency has designated the information as CUI. DOW's training is mandatory for any contractor who handles CUI. Be sure you take the test and keep a copy of the certificate (assuming you pass) at the end. Links to the DOW and NARA CUI training can be found at the end of this book.

For more details on CUI and the CUI program, the books *CUI Fundamentals* and *CUI Informed* by James Goepel (available from your favorite bookseller or https://CUIInformed.com) cover the CUI program in more detail than we can in this book.

CMMC Regulations

What is the purpose of CMMC?

The CMMC program is DOW's approach to ensuring that the federal government's sensitive information is properly protected when that information is given to, or created by, government contractors. This helps DOW meet its obligations under FAR 52.204-21, 32 CFR 2002.14(h)(2), and 32 CFR 2002.16(a)(4).

How has DOW's approach to CMMC changed over time?

When CMMC 1.0 was originally announced in 2019, it was envisioned as a set of internal policy memos and other documents that would guide Contracting Officers when they awarded a contract. In 2022, DOW conducted an internal review of the CMMC program and strengthened CMMC by adopting it as a set of formal regulations. These regulations are also referred to as "**rules**".

The formal rulemaking process for DOW's CMMC regulations has since played out. The first significant regulation, which established the CMMC program, became effective December 16, 2024.

The second significant regulation, which enables Contracting Officers to incorporate CMMC requirements into contracts and solicitations, was published in the Federal Register on September 10, 2025, and will become effective on November 10, 2025. This regulation also amends DFARS clauses 252.204-7012, 7019, 7020, and 7021.

Where is CMMC Program and related rules

As of the date of publication of this book, there are a total of four (4) different regulations that contractors should be aware of that are related to CMMC. Each of them is (or was) separately working its way through the rulemaking process, though, as noted below, there are certain interdependencies.

1. **CMMC Program** – On October 16, 2024, DOW published the final rule version of 32 CFR 170. That regulation formally established the CMMC program. The CMMC Program rule outlined the CMMC program and is the source of much of the information in this section of this book. The CMMC Program rule was effective as of December 16, 2024, and CMMC assessments permitted to begin as of that date.

However, CMMC requirements will not be incorporated into DOW contracts until the CMMC Acquisition rule is finalized.

2. **CMMC Acquisition** – The 48 CFR Final CMMC Rule was published in the Federal Register on September 10, 2025, and will become effective on November 10, 2025. This rule formally embeds the Cybersecurity Maturity Model Certification into the DFARS, transforming the once self-attestation framework into an enforceable contract requirement. It establishes CMMC Levels 1, 2, and 3 as binding standards for contractors and subcontractors handling FCI and CUI. The rule requires verification of certification status in the Supplier Performance Risk System (SPRS) before award, mandates annual affirmations, and enforces compliance through eligibility—no certification means no contract. It also introduces conditional certifications with strict limits, incorporates unique identifiers for covered systems, and removes outdated requirements such as reporting "lapses in information security" to contracting officers. The rule supplements DFARS clauses including 252.204-7012, 7019, 7020, modifies 7021 and establishes a new clause at 252.204-7025, fully integrating CMMC into the broader framework of acquisition regulations governing cybersecurity in the Defense Industrial Base.

3. **CUI and Incident Reporting** – DOW is updating DFARS 252.204- 7012 to make it consistent with the CMMC requirements, incident response requirements created by the White House, and to address other issues. This proposed rule is still being drafted and internally reviewed by DOW and has not been submitted to the White House for review. This is DFARS Case 2023-D024.

4. **FAR CUI Rule** – As discussed above, the CUI program was not created by DOW. It is a government-wide program which DOW and other federal agencies must follow. Unlike DOW, many federal agencies have been reluctant to adopt their own CUI programs, opting instead to wait until a government-wide set of policies and other requirements was created. NARA started working on the corresponding regulations in 2016, and on January 15, 2025, a proposed FAR rule on CUI was published in the Federal Register. The public comment period for this proposed rule concluded on March 17, 2025. While there is no official date for the finalization of the rule, it is anticipated that the final rule may be issued later in 2025.

Should I wait for all the CMMC-related rules to be finalized before beginning my CMMC journey?

No. And for several reasons.

First, our clients and partners consistently tell us that it takes 12-18 months (at a minimum) to fully implement the requirements in NIST SP 800-171. Given that CMMC Level 2 (Self), and even CMMC Level 2 (C3PAO), requirements will start appearing in contracts in November 2025, contractors need to start implementing the requirements now to avoid missing out on contracts. The next chapter (CMMC Program Questions) has more details on the CMMC implementation timeline.

Second, Contracting Officers are already able to award contracts based on your current score in SPRS. You can increase the odds of a successful award by ensuring that your proposal teammates and you all have (legitimate) high scores in SPRS.

Third, when DOW Contracting Officers create an RFP or RFI, they include not only a description of work to be performed or the goods to be purchased, but also a set of contract clauses which are pulled from the FAR and/or the DFARS. Regardless of whether these clauses are written out in full (i.e., expressly incorporated) or simply referenced in the contract (i.e., incorporated by reference), they become part of the contract with the government, and the contractor is obligated to meet those requirements.

The clause at FAR 52.204-21 is a required clause, meaning it must be incorporated into every government contract. This clause defines a basic set of information security protections that all contractors are expected to have in place. FAR 52.204-21 has been in effect since June 16, 2016.

In addition, the clause at DFARS 252.204-7012 requires that contractors who handle CUI implement NIST SP 800-171. This requirement has been in effect since 2017.

If you are a DOW contractor with an active contract, you likely have been contractually affirming that you meet these requirements. This carries with it significant risk if you are found to be noncompliant. Therefore, it is essential that you begin your compliance journey ASAP.

How does NIST SP 800-171 Rev. 3 play into all of this?

While NIST published NIST SP 800-171 Rev. 3 in May 2024, 32 CFR 170 indicates that, at the regulatory level, DOW has built CMMC around NIST SP 800-171 Rev. 2. This means that, at least for the time being, DOW contractors should focus on complying with NIST SP 800-171 Rev. 2. However, contractors would be wise to review Rev. 3 to ensure that any decisions made during their CMMC journey do not cause issues for them later when Rev. 3 (or a later version of NIST SP 800-171) is adopted as the requirement for CMMC.

Official Federal Resources

NIST FRAMEWORK DOCUMENTATION

NIST SP 800-171 Rev. 2

800-171 Rev. 2 - Framework including controls

https://csrc.nist.gov/pubs/sp/800/171/r2/upd1/final

800-171A - Assessment Guide

https://csrc.nist.gov/pubs/sp/800/171/a/final

NIST SP 800-171 Rev. 3

800-171 Rev. 3 - Framework including controls

https://csrc.nist.gov/pubs/sp/800/171/r3/final

800-171A Rev. 3 - Assessment Guide

https://csrc.nist.gov/pubs/sp/800/171/a/r3/final

NIST SP 800-172

Enhanced security requirements applicable to CMMC Level 3.

https://nvlpubs.nist.gov/nistpubs/SpecialPublications/NIST.SP.800-172.pdf

CUI DOCUMENTATION

32 CFR 2002 - CUI Program Implementing Regulation

The regulation which implements the CUI program across the entire Executive Branch.

https://www.ecfr.gov/current/title-32/subtitle-B/chapter-XX/part-2002

NARA CUI Registry

The authoritative list of CUI categories and related laws, regulations, and government-wide policies

https://archives/gov/CUI/registry/category-list

DoDI 5200.48 - DoD CUI Program

DoD Instruction which defines DoD's implementation of the CUI program.

https://www.esd.whs.mil/Portals/54/Documents/DD/issuances/dodi/520048p.PDF

DoD CUI Registry

Categories of CUI that may be encountered by DoD personnel and contractors

https://www.dodcui.mil/

NARA CUI Marking Handbook

Official methods for marking CUI

https://www.archives.gov/files/cui/documents/20161206-cui-marking-handbook-v1-1-20190524.pdf

FCI DOCUMENTATION

FAR 52.204-21

FCI – Security requirements to safeguard non-public federal contract information.

https://www.acquisition.gov/far/52.204-21

CMMC-RELATED REGULATIONS, MEMORANDA, AND GUIDANCE DOCUMENTS

CMMC Model, Scoping Guide, and Related Documents

Official CMMC DoD Materials

https://dodcio.defense.gov/CMMC/Resources-Documentation/

DoD Procurement Toolbox Cybersecurity FAQs

Expectations from the perspective of the contracting officer.

https://dodprocurementtoolbox.com/cms/sites/default/files/resources/2022-12/Cybersecurity%20FAQ%20update%2012-19-22.pdf

DoD Instruction 5230.24

DoD Distribution Statements – Everything you need know

https://www.esd.whs.mil/portals/54/documents/dd/issuances/dodi/523024p.pdf

DFARS 252.204-7012

Primary regulation for Covered Defense Information and Cyber Incident Reporting. Clauses (c)-(g) include requirements going beyond CMMC.

https://www.acquisition.gov/dfars/252.204-7012-safeguarding-covered-defense-information-and-cyber-incident-reporting.

DFARS 252.204-7019

Notice of DoD Cyber-Assessment Requirements to be considered for award.

https://www.acquisition.gov/dfars/252.204-7019-notice-nistsp-800-171-dod-assessment-requirements.

DFARS 252.204-7020

Requires contractors to provide the Government with access.

https://www.acquisition.gov/dfars/252.204-7020-nist-sp-800-171dod-assessment-requirements.

DFARS 252.204-7021

CMMC-Specific DoD Cyber-Assessment Requirements

https://www.acquisition.gov/dfars/252.204-7021-cybersecurity-maturity-model-certification-requirements.

DFARS 252.204-7024

Regulation re: the use of the SPRS Score in contract decisions.

https://www.acquisition.gov/dfars/252.204-7024-notice-use-supplier-performance-risk-system.

SPRS Factsheet

Basic expectations and explanation of SPRS

https://www.acq.osd.mil/asda/dpc/cp/cyber/docs/safeguarding/SPRS_FactSheet.pdf

DoD Assessment Methodology

The scoring approach used for SPRS submissions.

https://www.acq.osd.mil/asda/dpc/cp/cyber/docs/safeguarding/NIST-SP-800-171-Assessment-Methodology-Version-1.2.1-6.24.2020.pdf

Key CMMC Tools and Resources

Advisory and Training Resources

***NIST Manufacturing Extension Partnerships**

Assistance to manufacturers. May include financial and advisory resources.

https://www.nist.gov/mep/cybersecurity-resources-manufacturers

***APEX Accelerators**

(formerly the Procurement Technical Assistance Program)

Assistance to manufacturers. May include financial and advisory resources.

https://www.apexaccelerators.us/

United States Air Force Blue Cyber Education Series for Small Business

https://www.safcn.af.mil/CISO/Small-Business-Cybersecurity-Information/

Mandatory DoD CUI Training

This course is mandatory training for all DoD personnel with access to controlled unclassified information.

https://securityawareness.usalearning.gov/cui/index.html

Project Spectrum

Free government-backed website with very basic CMMC compliance training and tools.

https://www.projectspectrum.io/#/

CCP and CCA Licensed Training Provider

SMU offers both CCP and CCA programs as a CAICO LTP.
CCP: https://www.smu.edu/CAPE/Programs/Certificates/CCP
CCA: https://www.smu.edu/CAPE/Programs/Certificates/CCA

The CMMC Information Institute

Non-profit resource with up-to-the minute definitive information regarding CMMC, CUI, and more.

https://CMMCInfo.org

15 Minutes with FutureFeed

No cost resource available weekly to provide answers regarding CMMC implementation from Cyber AB certified professionals.

https://FutureFeed.co/15

* May have financial resources available depending upon state and business standing.

CMMC Official Resources

The Cyber AB

The accreditation body for CMMC. Definitive information about the assessment process and the training and certification programs that support it.

https://CyberAB.org

Cyber AB – Licensed Training Providers

Find an officially licensed training provider for staff certifications.

https://cyberab.org/Catalog#!/c/s/Results/Format/list/Page/1/Size/9/Sort/NameAscending?typeId=10

SMU LTP Listing:

https://cyberab.org/Catalog#!/c/s/Results/Format/list/Page/1/Size/9/Sort/NameAscending?term=southern%20methodist%20university

Cyber AB – Official C3PAO (Assessment Organization) Listing

Find a list of authorized C3PAOs to conduct an official assessment.

https://cyberab.org/Catalog#!/c/s/Results/Format/list/Page/1/Size/9/Sort/NameAscending?typeId=7

Cyber AB – Registered Provider Organizations (RPOs)

Find a list of organizations which have committed significant resources to participate in the CMMC ecosystem and which can help you create your CMMC compliance program.

https://cyberab.org/Catalog#!/c/s/Results/Format/list/Page/1/Size/9/Sort/NameAscending?typeId=3

CMMC Program Rule (Final)

The final CMMC Program Rule.

https://www.federalregister.gov/d/2024-22905/p-amd-1

CMMC Program Rule – Guidance Documents

The official CMMC model overview, scoping, assessment, and hashing guides, along with links to other resources.

https://dodcio.defense.gov/CMMC/Resources-Documentation/

Government Reporting Requirements

DoD Cyber Crime Center (DC3) Defense Industrial Base (DIB) Cybersecurity Program

DCISE is the operational hub of the Defense Industrial Base (DIB) Cybersecurity Program of the Department of War, focused on protecting intellectual property and safeguarding DoD content residing on, or transiting through, contractor unclassified networks.

https://www.dc3.mil/Missions/DIB-Cybersecurity/DIB-Cybersecurity-DCISE/

DIBNet Portal

Mandatory portal to report cyber-incidents. Registration, approval, and certificates issued in advance required for use.

https://dibnet.dod.mil/dibnet/

SPRS Portal

Report NIST SP 800-171 compliance scores on this site, operated by the Navy, and often required to qualify for contracts and to operate as a subcontractor for DoD contracts that include a DFARS clause. Registration and approval required for use.

https://www.sprs.csd.disa.mil/

Useful DoD Official Presentations

CMMC Alignment to NIST Standards
How the Requirements Fit into the Assessment Framework
February 2025

Use this PowerPoint presentation when you're getting started with CMMC compliance and need to understand how your efforts align with NIST standards. It's especially helpful when:

- Planning your approach to meet CMMC Level 2 requirements
- Preparing for a self-assessment or C3PAO audit
- Updating your SSP or POA&Ms
- Deciding whether to begin transitioning to NIST SP 800-171 Rev. 3

https://dodcio.defense.gov/Portals/0/Documents/CMMC/CMMC-AlignmentNIST-Standards.pdf

FedRAMP Authorization and Equivalency
Cloud Requirements for the Defense Industrial Base
February 2025

Use this PowerPoint presentation when you're evaluating or using cloud services to store, process, or transmit Covered Defense Information (CDI). It's especially helpful when:

- You need to understand DFARS 252.204-7012 cloud requirements
- You're considering FedRAMP-authorized vs. FedRAMP-equivalent solutions
- You're preparing a Body of Evidence for DIBCAC or a C3PAO
- You want to ensure your CSP meets DoD's FedRAMP Moderate Equivalency expectations

https://dodcio.defense.gov/Portals/0/Documents/CMMC/FedRAMP-AuthorizationEquivalency.pdf

Technical Application of CMMC Requirements
ESPs, Asset Categories, SPA/SPD, and VDI
February 2025

Use this PowerPoint presentation when you're defining the technical boundaries of your CMMC environment. It's especially helpful when:

- Scoping External Service Providers (ESPs), like MSPs, MSSPs, and CSPs
- Determining if cloud services meet FedRAMP or equivalency requirements
- Categorizing assets (SPA, SPD, CRMA, VDI, Specialized) for Level 2 or Level 3
- Preparing your SSP, asset inventory, and network diagram for C3PAO or DIBCAC review

https://dodcio.defense.gov/Portals/0/Documents/CMMC/TechImplementationCMMC-Rqrmnts.pdf

Introduction to the CMMC Enterprise Mission Assurance Support Service (eMASS)
February 12, 2025

Use this PowerPoint presentation when you're defining the technical boundaries of your CMMC environment. It's especially helpful when:

- Scoping External Service Providers (ESPs), like MSPs, MSSPs, and CSPs
- Determining if cloud services meet FedRAMP or equivalency requirements
- Categorizing assets (SPA, SPD, CRMA, VDI, Specialized) for Level 2 or Level 3
- Preparing your SSP, asset inventory, and network diagram for C3PAO or DIBCAC review

https://dodcio.defense.gov/Portals/0/Documents/CMMC/CMMC-eMASS.pdf

CMMC Level Determination
December 23, 2024

Use this PowerPoint presentation when you're determining which CMMC level applies to your contract. It's especially helpful when:

- You're deciding whether CMMC Level 2 is required for your organization
- You need to distinguish between Self-Assessment and Certification pathways for Level 2
- You handle Controlled Unclassified Information (CUI) and must assess its classification based on the NARA Registry and Defense OIG designation

https://dodcio.defense.gov/Portals/0/Documents/CMMC/CMMC-LevelsDeterminationBrief.pdf

DoD Regulatory Memorandums

MEMORANDUM FOR SENIOR PENTAGON LEADERSHIP DEFENSE AGENCY AND DOD FIELD ACTIVITY DIRECTORS
January 15, 2025

Implementing the Cybersecurity Maturity Model Certification (CMMC) Program: Guidance for Detemlining Appropriate CMMC Compliance Assessment Levels and Process for Waiving CMMC Assessment Requirements

- Use this memo when you're determining which CMMC level to apply to a contract or evaluating whether a waiver from CMMC requirements is appropriate. It's especially helpful when:
- You're a Program Manager or Acquisition Executive selecting CMMC levels during procurement planning
- You're deciding between self-assessment or third-party certification for Level 2
- You're evaluating if enhanced protections (Level 3) are needed
- You're requesting or reviewing a CMMC assessment waiver under defined conditions

https://dodprocurementtoolbox.com/uploads/DOPSR_Cleared_OSD_Memo_CMMC_Implementation_Policy_d26075de0f.pdf

Tools and Financial Services

FutureFeed

Leading Cyber-GRC platform, focused on NIST SP 800-171 / CMMC Compliance. Micro-training and starter templates built in.

https://FutureFeed.co

Parabilis

Working capital financing for government contractors (especially with cyber-compliance funding needs).

https://Parabilis.com

CISA

Free cybersecurity tools and services

https://www.cisa.gov/resources-tools/resources/free-cybersecurity-services-and-tools

Acronyms and Glossary

Acronyms*	
3PAO	FedRAMP Authorized 3rd Party Assessment Organization
AC	Access Control
APT	Advanced Persistent Threat
AT	Awareness and Training
ATO	Authority to Operate
C3	Cybersecurity Collaboration Center at NSA
C3PAO	CMMC 3rd Party Assessment Organization
CA	Security Assessment
CAGE	Commercial and Government Entity code
CAICO	CMMC Assessors and Instructors Certification Organization
CCA	CMMC-Certified Assessor
CCI	CMMC-Certified Instructor
CCP	CMMC-Certified Professional
CDI	Covered Defense Information
CEIC	CMMC Ecosystem Summit + CMMC Implementation Conferences
CFR	Code of Federal Regulations
CIO	Chief Information Officer
CISA	Cybersecurity and Infrastructure Security Agency
CM	Configuration Management
CMMC	Cybersecurity Maturity Model Certification
CMMC PMO	CMMC Program Management Office
CNC	Computerized Numerical Control
CoPC	Code of Professional Conduct
CRM	Customer Responsibility Matrix
CRMA	Contractor Risk Managed Asset
CSP	Cloud Service Provider
CUI	Controlled Unclassified Information
CVE	Common Vulnerabilities and Exposures
CVSS	Common Vulnerability Scoring System
DCMA	Defense Contract Management Agency
DC3	DoD Cyber Crime Center

DD	Represents any two-character CMMC Domain acronym
DFARS	Defense Federal Acquisition Regulations Supplement
DIB	Defense Industrial Base
DIBCAC	DCMA's Defense Industrial Base Cybersecurity Assessment Center
DOW	Department of War
DoDAM	DoD Assessment Methodology
DoDI	Department of Defense Instruction
DoJ	United States Department of Justice
eMASS	Enterprise Mission Assurance Support Service
ESP	External Service Provider
FAR	Federal Acquisition Regulations
FCI	Federal Contract Information
FedRAMP	Federal Risk and Authorization Management Program
FIPS	Federal Information Processing Standards
FISMA	Federal Information Security Modernization Act
FOIA	Freedom of Information Act
FOUO	For Official Use Only
GFE	Government Furnished Equipment
IA	Identification and Authentication
IaaS	Infrastructure as a Service
ICS	Industrial Control System
IEC	International Electromechanical Commission
IIoT	Industrial Internet of Things
IoT	Internet of Things
IR	Incident Response
IS	Information System
ISO/IEC	International Organization for Standardization/International Electrotechnical Commission
ISOO	Information Security Oversight Office
IT	Information Technology
ITAR	International Traffic in Arms Regulations
JSVA	Joint Surveillance Voluntary Assessment
L#	CMMC Level Number
LES	Law Enforcement Sensitive
LPP	Licensed Publishing Partner

LRGWP	Law, Regulation, or Government-Wide Policy
LTP	Licensed Training Provider
MA	Maintenance
MEP	Manufacturing Extension Partnership
MP	Media Protection
MSP	Managed (IT) Service Provider
MSSP	Managed Security Service Provider
NARA	National Archives and Records Administration
NAICS	North American Industry Classification System
NIST	National Institute of Standards and Technology
NSA	National Security Agency
NVD	National Vulnerability Database
N/A	Not Applicable
ODP	Organization-Defined Parameter
OSA	Organization Seeking Assessment
OSC	Organization Seeking Certification
OT	Operational Technology
PaaS	Platform as a Service
PCI	Payment Card Industry
PDNS	Protective Domain Name System
PIEE	Procurement Integrated Enterprise Environment
PII	Personally Identifiable Information
PLC	Programmable Logic Controller
POA&M	Plan of Action and Milestones
PRA	Paperwork Reduction Act
RFI	Request for Information
RFP	Request for Proposal
RM	Risk Management
RP	Registered Practitioner
RPA	Registered Practitioner Advanced
RPO	Registered Provider Organization
SaaS	Software as a Service
SAM	System of Award Management
SBA	Small Business Administration
SBU	Sensitive but Unclassified
SC	System and Communications Protection
SCADA	Supervisory Control and Data Acquisition
SCAP	Security Content Automation Protocol
SCG	Security Classification Guide
SCRM	Supply Chain Risk Management

SI	System and Information Integrity
SIEM	Security Information and Event Management
SP	Special Publication
SPA	Security Protection Asset
SPD	Security Protection Data
SPRS	Supplier Performance Risk System
SRM	Replaced by CRM (Shared Responsibility Matrix)
SSP	System Security Plan
VDI	Virtual Desktop Interface

* Curated from NIST SP 800-171 Rev. 2, 32 CFR Part 170, and other sources.

Glossary*

Access Control	The process of granting or denying specific requests to obtain and use information and related information processing services; and/or entry to specific physical facilities (e.g., Federal buildings, military establishments, or border crossing entrances), as defined in FIPS PUB 201-3 Jan2002
Accreditation	A status pursuant to which a CMMC Assessment and Certification Ecosystem member (person or organization), having met all criteria for the specific role they perform including required ISO/IEC accreditations, may act in that role as set forth in § 170.8 for the Accreditation Body and § 170.9 for C3PAOs.
Accreditation Body	The one organization DoD contracts with to be responsible for authorizing and accrediting members of the CMMC Assessment and Certification Ecosystem, as required. The Accreditation Body must be approved by DoD. At any given point in time, there will be only one Accreditation Body for the DoD CMMC Program.
Agency	Any executive agency or department, military department, Federal Government corporation, Federal Government-controlled corporation, or other establishment in the Executive Branch of the Federal Government, or any independent regulatory agency.
Advanced Persistent Threat	An adversary that possesses sophisticated levels of expertise and significant resources that allow it to create opportunities to achieve its objectives by using multiple attack vectors (e.g., cyber, physical, and deception). These objectives typically include establishing and extending footholds within the information technology infrastructure of the targeted organizations for purposes of exfiltrating information, undermining or impeding critical aspects of a mission, program, or organization; or positioning itself to carry out these objectives in the future. The advanced persistent threat pursues its objectives repeatedly over an extended period-of-time, adapts to defenders' efforts to resist it, and is determined to maintain the level of interaction needed to execute its objectives, as is defined in NIST SP 800-39 Mar2011
Affirming Official	The senior level representative from within each Organization Seeking Assessment (OSA) who is responsible for ensuring the OSA's compliance with the

	CMMC Program requirements and has the authority to affirm the OSA's continuing compliance with the specified security requirements for their respective organizations.
Assessment	The testing or evaluation of security controls to determine the extent to which the controls are implemented correctly, operating as intended, and producing the desired outcome with respect to meeting the security requirements for an information system or organization, as defined in §§ 170.15 through 170.18.
Assessment Findings Report	The final written assessment results by the third-party or government assessment team. The Assessment Findings Report is submitted to the OSC and to the DoD via CMMC eMASS.
Assessment Objective	a set of determination statements that, taken together, expresses the desired outcome for the assessment of a security requirement. Successful implementation of the corresponding CMMC security requirement requires meeting all applicable assessment objectives defined in NIST SP 800-171A Jun2018 (incorporated by reference, see § 170.2) or NIST SP 800-172A Mar2022 (incorporated by reference, see § 170.2).
Assessment Scope	See *CMMC Assessment Scope*
Assessment Team	Participants in the Level 2 certification assessment (CMMC Certified Assessors and CMMC Certified Professionals) or the Level 3 certification assessment (DCMA DIBCAC assessors). This does not include the OSC participants preparing for or participating in the assessment.
Assessor	See *security control assessor.*
Asset	An item of value to stakeholders. An asset may be tangible (e.g., a physical item such as hardware, firmware, computing platform, network device, or other technology component) or intangible ((e.g. humans, data, information, software, capability, function, service, trademark, copyright, patent, intellectual property, image, or reputation). The value of an asset is determined by stakeholders in consideration of loss concerns across the entire system life cycle. Such concerns include but are not limited to business or mission concerns, as defined in NIST SP 800-160 V2R1 (incorporated by reference, see § 170.2).

Asset Categories	A grouping of assets that process, store or transmit information of similar designation, or provide security protection to those assets.
Audit Log	A chronological record of system activities, including records of system accesses and operations performed in a given period.
Authentication	Verifying the identity of a user, process, or device, often as a prerequisite to allowing access to resources in a system.
Authorized	An interim status during which a CMMC Ecosystem member (person or organization), having met all criteria for the specific role they perform other than the required ISO/IEC accreditations, may act in that role for a specified time as set forth in § 170.8 for the Accreditation Body and § 170.9 for C3PAOs.
Availability	Ensuring timely and reliable access to and use of information.
Authenticator	Something the claimant possesses and controls (typically a cryptographic module or password) that is used to authenticate the claimant's identity. This was previously referred to as a token.
Baseline Configuration	A documented set of specifications for a system or a configuration item within a system that has been formally reviewed and agreed upon at a given point in time, and that can only be changed through change control procedures.
Capability	A combination of mutually reinforcing controls implemented by technical means, physical means, and procedural means. Such controls are typically selected to achieve a common information security or privacy purpose, as defined in NIST SP 800-37 R2 (incorporated by reference, see 32 CFR § 170.2).
Cloud Service Provider	An external company that provides cloud services based on cloud computing. Cloud computing is a model for enabling ubiquitous, convenient, on-demand network access to a shared pool of configurable computing resources (e.g., networks, servers, storage, applications, and services) that can be rapidly provisioned and released with minimal management effort or service provider interaction. This definition is based on the definition for cloud computing in NIST SP 800-145 Sept2011

CMMC Assessment and Certification Ecosystem	The people and organizations described in subpart C of 32 CFR 170. This term is sometimes shortened to CMMC Ecosystem.
CMMC Assessment Scope	The set of all assets in the OSA's environment that will be assessed against CMMC security requirements.
CMMC Assessor and Instructor Certification Organization	The organization responsible for training, testing, authorizing, certifying, and recertifying CMMC certified assessors, certified instructors, and certified professionals.
CMMC Instantiation of eMASS	A CMMC instance of the Enterprise Mission Assurance Support Service (eMASS), a government owned and operated system.
CMMC Security Requirements	The 15 Level 1 requirements listed in the 48 CFR 52.204-21(b)(1), the 110 Level 2 requirements from NIST SP 800-171 R2 (incorporated by reference, see 32 CFR § 170.2), and the 24 Level 3 requirements selected from NIST SP 800-172 Feb2021
CMMC Status	The result of meeting or exceeding the minimum required score for the corresponding assessment. The CMMC Status of an OSA information system is officially stored in SPRS and additionally presented on a Certificate of CMMC Status, if the assessment was conducted by a C3PAO or DCMA DIBCAC.
CMMC Status Date	The date that the CMMC Status results are submitted to SPRS or the CMMC instantiation of eMASS, as appropriate. The date of the Conditional CMMC Status will remain as the CMMC Status Date after a successful POA&M closeout. A new date is not set for a Final that follows a Conditional.
CMMC Third-Party Assessment Organization	An organization that has been authorized or accredited by the Accreditation Body to conduct Level 2 certification assessments and has the roles and responsibilities identified in 32 CFR § 170.9

Common Secure Configuration	Recognized, standardized, and established benchmarks that stipulate secure configuration settings for specific information technology platforms/products and instructions for configuring those system components to meet operational requirements. These benchmarks are also referred to as security configuration checklists, lockdown and hardening guides, security reference guides, and security technical implementation guides.
Confidentiality	Preserving authorized restrictions on information access and disclosure, including means for protecting personal privacy and proprietary information.
Configuration Management	A collection of activities focused on establishing and maintaining the integrity of information technology products and systems through the control of processes for initializing, changing, and monitoring the configurations of those products and systems throughout the system development life cycle.
Configuration Settings	The set of parameters that can be changed in hardware, software, or firmware that affect the security posture and/or functionality of the system.
Controlled Area	Any area or space for which the organization has confidence that the physical and procedural protections provided are sufficient to meet the requirements established for protecting the information or system.
Controlled Environment	Any area or space an authorized holder deems to have adequate physical or procedural controls (e.g., barriers or managed access controls) to protect CUI from unauthorized access or disclosure.
Controlled Unclassified Information	Information the Government creates or possesses, or that an entity creates or possesses for or on behalf of the Government, that a law, regulation, or Government-wide policy requires or permits an agency to handle using safeguarding or dissemination controls. However, CUI does not include classified information (see definition above) or information a non-executive branch entity possesses and maintains in its own systems that did not come from, or was not created or possessed by or for, an executive branch agency or an entity acting for an agency. Law, regulation, or Government-wide policy may require or permit safeguarding or dissemination controls in three ways: Requiring or permitting agencies to control or protect the information but providing no specific controls, which makes the information CUI Basic; requiring or permitting

	agencies to control or protect the information and providing specific controls for doing so, which makes the information CUI Specified; or requiring or permitting agencies to control the information and specifying only some of those controls, which makes the information CUI Specified, but with CUI Basic controls where the authority does not specify.
Controlled Unclassified Information (CUI) Assets	Assets that can process, store, or transmit CUI.
Controls	Safeguarding or dissemination controls that a law, regulation, or Government-wide policy requires or permits agencies to use when handling CUI. The authority may specify the controls it requires or permits the agency to apply, or the authority may generally require or permit agencies to control the information (in which case, the agency applies the controls from Executive Order 13556, 32 CFR Part 2002, and the CUI Registry).
CUI Basic	The subset of CUI for which the authorizing law, regulation, or Government-wide policy does not set out specific handling or dissemination controls. Agencies handle CUI Basic according to the uniform set of controls set forth in this part and the CUI Registry. CUI Basic differs from CUI Specified (see definition for CUI Specified), and CUI Basic controls apply whenever CUI Specified ones do not cover the involved CUI.
CUI Executive Agent	The National Archives and Records Administration (NARA), which implements the executive branch-wide CUI Program and oversees federal agency actions to comply with Executive Order 13556. NARA has delegated this authority to the Director of the Information Security Oversight Office (ISOO).
CUI Program	The executive branch-wide program to standardize CUI handling by all federal agencies. The program includes the rules, organization, and procedures for CUI, established by Executive Order 13556, 32 CFR Part 2002, and the CUI Registry.
CUI Registry	The online repository for all information, guidance, policy, and requirements on handling CUI, including everything issued by the CUI Executive Agent other than 32 CFR Part 2002. Among other information, the CUI Registry identifies all approved CUI categories and subcategories, provides

	general descriptions for each, identifies the basis for controls, establishes markings, and includes guidance on handling procedures.
CUI Specified	The subset of CUI in which the authorizing law, regulation, or Government-wide policy contains specific handling controls that it requires or permits agencies to use that differ from those for CUI Basic. The CUI Registry indicates which laws, regulations, and Government-wide policies include such specific requirements. CUI Specified controls may be more stringent than, or may simply differ from, those required by CUI Basic; the distinction is that the underlying authority spells out the controls for CUI Specified information and does not for CUI Basic information. CUI Basic controls apply to those aspects of CUI Specified where the authorizing laws, regulations, and Government-wide policies do not provide specific guidance.
Customer Responsibility	The obligations of an organization to implement and manage specific security and operational controls that are not handled by the external service provider.
Customer Responsibility Matrix	A tool used to delineate and document the specific security responsibilities between an organization and its external service providers (ESPs), such as cloud service providers (CSPs) or managed service providers (MSPs). This matrix ensures that both parties clearly understand their obligations concerning the implementation and management of security controls, particularly in frameworks like NIST 800-171 and NIST 800-53.
Cyber-Physical Systems	Interacting digital, analog, physical, and human components engineered for function through integrated physics and logic.
DCMA DIBCAC High Assessment	An assessment that is conducted by Government personnel in accordance with NIST SP 800-171A Jun2018 and leveraging specific guidance in the DoD Assessment Methodology that: (i) Consists of: (A) A review of a contractor's Basic Assessment; (B) A thorough document review; (C) Verification, examination, and demonstration of a contractor's system security plan to validate that NIST SP 800-171 R2 security requirements have been implemented as described in the contractor's system security plan; and

	(D) Discussions with the contractor to obtain additional information or clarification, as needed; and (ii) Results in a confidence level of "High" in the resulting score. (Source: 48 CFR 252.204-7020).
Debarred	Excluded from receiving contracts. Agencies are prohibited from soliciting offers from, awarding contracts to, or consenting to subcontracts with these contractors, unless the agency head determines that there is a compelling reason for such action. Contractors debarred, suspended, or proposed for debarment are also excluded from conducting business with the Government as agents or representatives of other contractors or as subcontractors.
DoD Assessment Methodology	Documents a standard methodology that enables a strategic assessment of a contractor's implementation of NIST SP 800-171 R2, a requirement for compliance with 48 CFR 252.204-7012. The DoD Assessment Methodology can be found at https://www.acq.osd.mil/asda/dpc/cp/cyber/docs/safeguarding/NIST-SP-800-171-Assessment-Methodology-Version-1.2.1-6.24.2020.pdf.
Enduring Exception	A special circumstance or system where remediation and full compliance with CMMC security requirements is not feasible. Examples include systems required to replicate the configuration of 'fielded' systems, medical devices, test equipment, OT, and IoT. No operational plan of action is required but the circumstance must be documented within a system security plan. Specialized Assets and GFE may be enduring exceptions.
Enterprise	An organization with a defined mission/goal and a defined boundary, using information systems to execute that mission, and with responsibility for managing its own risks and performance. An enterprise may consist of all or some of the following business aspects: acquisition, program management, financial management (e.g., budgets), human resources, security, and information systems, information and mission management, as defined in NIST SP 800-53 R5.
Executive Agency	An executive department specified in 5 U.S.C. Sec. 101; a military department specified in 5 U.S.C. Sec. 102; an independent establishment as defined in 5 U.S.C. Sec. 104(1); and a wholly owned Government corporation fully subject to the provisions of 31 U.S.C. Chapter 91.

External Network	A network not controlled by the organization.
External Service Provider	External people, technology, or facilities that an organization utilizes for provision and management of IT and/or cybersecurity services on behalf of the organization. In the CMMC Program, CUI or Security Protection Data (e.g., log data, configuration data), must be processed, stored, or transmitted on the ESP assets to be considered an ESP.
External System (or Component)	A system or component of a system that is outside of the authorization boundary established by the organization and for which the organization typically has no direct control over the application of required security controls or the assessment of security control effectiveness.
External System Service	A system service that is implemented outside of the authorization boundary of the organizational system (i.e., a service that is used by but not a part of the organizational system) and for which the organization typically has no direct control over the application of required security controls or the assessment of security control effectiveness.
External System Service Provider	A provider of external system services to an organization through a variety of consumer-producer relationships, including joint ventures, business partnerships, outsourcing arrangements (i.e., through contracts, interagency agreements, lines of business arrangements), licensing agreements, and/or supply chain exchanges.
Facility	One or more physical locations containing systems or system components that process, store, or transmit information.
Federal Agency	See *executive agency*.
Federal Contract Information	Information, not intended for public release, that is provided by or generated for the Government under a contract to develop or deliver a product or service to the Government, but not including information provided by the Government to the public (such as that on public Web sites) or simple transactional information, such as that necessary to process payments.

Federal Information System	An information system used or operated by an executive agency, by a contractor of an executive agency, or by another organization on behalf of an executive agency.
Fielded Device	Equipment that is connected to the field side on an ICS. Types of field devices include RTUs, PLCs, actuators, sensors, HMIs, and associated communications.
FIPS-Validated Cryptography	A cryptographic module validated by the Cryptographic Module Validation Program (CMVP) to meet the requirements specified in FIPS Publication 140-3 (as amended). As a prerequisite to CMVP validation, the cryptographic module is required to employ a cryptographic algorithm implementation that has successfully passed validation testing by the Cryptographic Algorithm Validation Program (CAVP). See *NSA-approved cryptography*
Firmware	Computer programs and data stored in hardware – typically in read-only memory (ROM) or programmable read-only memory (PROM) – such that the programs and data cannot be dynamically written or modified during execution of the programs. See *hardware* and *software*.
Flow Down	A flow down clause is a contract provision by which the parties incorporate the terms of the general contract between the owner and the prime contractor into the lower tier agreement. It may also be referred to as a pass-through or conduit clause. Such provisions state that the subcontractor is bound to the contractor in the same manner as the contractor is bound to the owner in the prime contract. Flow-down provisions help to ensure that the subcontractor's obligations to the contractor mirror the contractor's obligations to the owner.
Government Furnished Equipment	Property in the possession of, or directly acquired by, the Government and subsequently furnished to the contractor for performance of a contract. Government-furnished property includes, but is not limited to, spares and property furnished for repair, maintenance, overhaul, or modification. Government-furnished property also includes contractor-acquired property if the contractor-acquired property is a deliverable under a cost contract when accepted by the Government for continued use under the contract.
Hardware	The material physical components of a system. See *software* and *firmware*.

Identifier	Unique data used to represent a person's identity and associated attributes. A name or a card number are examples of identifiers. A unique label used by a system to indicate a specific entity, object, or group.
Impact	With respect to security, the effect on organizational operations, organizational assets, individuals, other organizations, or the Nation (including the national security interests of the United States) of a loss of confidentiality, integrity, or availability of information or a system. With respect to privacy, the adverse effects that individuals could experience when an information system processes their PII.
Impact Value	The assessed worst-case potential impact that could result from a compromise of the confidentiality, integrity, or availability of information expressed as a value of low, moderate, or high.
Incident	An occurrence that actually or imminently jeopardizes, without lawful authority, the confidentiality, integrity, or availability of information or an information system; or constitutes a violation or imminent threat of violation of law, security policies, security procedures, or acceptable use policies.
Industrial Control systems	A general term that encompasses several types of control systems, including supervisory control and data acquisition (SCADA) systems, distributed control systems (DCS), and other control system configurations that are often found in the industrial sectors and critical infrastructures, such as Programmable Logic Controllers (PLC). An ICS consists of combinations of control components (e.g., electrical, mechanical, hydraulic, pneumatic) that act together to achieve an industrial objective ((e.g. manufacturing, transportation of matter or energy), as defined in NIST SP 800-82r3
Information	Any communication or representation of knowledge such as facts, data, or opinions in any medium or form, including textual, numerical, graphic, cartographic, narrative, electronic, or audiovisual forms.
Information Flow Control	Procedure to ensure that information transfers within a system do not violate the security policy.

Information Resources	Information and related resources, such as personnel, equipment, funds, and information technology.
Information Security	The protection of information and systems from unauthorized access, use, disclosure, disruption, modification, or destruction in order to provide confidentiality, integrity, and availability.
Information System	A discrete set of information resources organized for the collection, processing, maintenance, use, sharing, dissemination, or disposition of information.
Information Technology	Any services, equipment, or interconnected system(s) or subsystem(s) of equipment, that are used in the automatic acquisition, storage, analysis, evaluation, manipulation, management, movement, control, display, switching, interchange, transmission, or reception of data or information by the agency. For purposes of this definition, such services or equipment if used by the agency directly or is used by a contractor under a contract with the agency that requires its use, or to a significant extent, its use in the performance of a service or the furnishing of a product. Information technology includes computers, ancillary equipment (including imaging peripherals, input, output, and storage devices necessary for security and surveillance), peripheral equipment designed to be controlled by the central processing unit of a computer, software, firmware and similar procedures, services (including cloud computing and help-desk services or other professional services which support any point of the life cycle of the equipment or service), and related resources. Information technology does not include any equipment that is acquired by a contractor incidental to a contract which does not require its use.
Insider Threat	The threat that an insider will use her/his authorized access, wittingly or unwittingly, to do harm to the security of the United States. This threat can include damage to the United States through espionage, terrorism, unauthorized disclosure, or through the loss or degradation of departmental resources or capabilities.
Integrity	Guarding against improper information modification or destruction and includes ensuring information non-repudiation and authenticity.
Internal Network	A network in which the establishment, maintenance, and provisioning of security controls are under the direct control of organizational employees or contractors or in

	which the cryptographic encapsulation or similar security technology implemented between organization-controlled endpoints provides the same effect (with regard to confidentiality and integrity). An internal network is typically organization-owned yet may be organization-controlled while not being organization-owned.
Internet of Things	The network of devices that contain the hardware, software, firmware, and actuators which allow the devices to connect, interact, and freely exchange data and information, as defined in NIST SP 800-172A Mar2022.
Least Privilege	The principle that a security architecture is designed so that each entity is granted the minimum system authorizations and resources needed to perform its function.
Lawful Government Purpose	Any activity, mission, function, operation, or endeavor that the U.S. Government authorizes or recognizes within the scope of its legal authorities or the legal authorities of non-executive branch entities (such as state and local law enforcement).
Malicious Code	Software or firmware intended to perform an unauthorized process that will have an adverse impact on the confidentiality, integrity, or availability of a system. Examples of malicious code include viruses, worms, Trojan horses, spyware, some forms of adware, or other code-based entities that infect a host.
Media	Physical devices or writing surfaces including, but not limited to, magnetic tapes, optical disks, magnetic disks, Large-Scale Integration (LSI) memory chips, and printouts (but not including display media) onto which information is recorded, stored, or printed within a system.
Mobile Code	Software programs or parts of programs obtained from remote systems, transmitted across a network, and executed on a local system without explicit installation or execution by the recipient.
Mobile Device	A portable computing device that has a small form factor such that it can easily be carried by a single individual; is designed to operate without a physical connection (e.g., wirelessly transmit or receive information); possesses local, non-removable, or removable data storage; and includes a self-contained power source. Mobile devices may also include voice communication capabilities, on-board sensors that allow the devices to capture

	information, or built-in features that synchronize local data with remote locations. Examples include smartphones, tablets, and e-readers.
Multi-Factor Authentication	Authentication using two or more different factors to achieve authentication. Factors include something you know (e.g., PIN, password), something you have (e.g., cryptographic identification device, token), or something you are (e.g., biometric). See *authenticator*.
Network	A system implemented with a collection of interconnected components. Such components may include routers, hubs, cabling, telecommunications controllers, key distribution centers, and technical control devices.
Network Access	Access to a system by a user (or a process acting on behalf of a user) communicating through a network (e.g., local area network, wide area network, the internet).
Nonfederal Organization	An entity that owns, operates, or maintains a nonfederal system.
Nonfederal System	A system that does not meet the criteria for a federal system
Nonlocal Maintenance	Maintenance activities conducted by individuals communicating through an external network (e.g., the internet) or an internal network.
NSA-Approved Cryptography	Cryptography that consists of an approved algorithm, an implementation that has been approved for the protection of classified information and/or controlled unclassified information in a specific environment, and a supporting key management infrastructure.
On behalf of (an agency)	A situation that occurs when: (i) a non-executive branch entity uses or operates an information system or maintains or collects information for the purpose of processing, storing, or transmitting Federal information; and (ii)those activities are not incidental to providing a service or product to the government.
Operational Plan of Action	As used in security requirement CA.L2-3.12.2, means the formal artifact which identifies temporary vulnerabilities and temporary deficiencies (e.g., necessary information system updates, patches, or reconfiguration as threats evolve) in implementation of requirements and documents how they will be mitigated, corrected, or eliminated. The

	OSA defines the format (*e.g.*, document, spreadsheet, database) and specific content of its operational plan of action. An operational plan of action does not identify a timeline for remediation and is not the same as a POA&M, which is associated with an assessment for remediation of deficiencies that must be completed within 180 days.
Operational Technology	Programmable systems or devices that interact with the physical environment (or manage devices that interact with the physical environment). These systems or devices detect or cause a direct change through the monitoring or control of devices, processes, and events. Examples include industrial control systems, building management systems, fire control systems, and physical access control mechanisms, as defined in NIST SP 800-160 V2R1.
Organization	An entity of any size, complexity, or positioning within an organizational structure.
Organization-Defined	As determined by the OSA except as defined in the case of Organization-Defined Parameter (ODP).
Organization-Defined Parameter	Selected enhanced security requirements contain selection and assignment operations to give organizations flexibility in defining variable parts of those requirements, as defined in NIST SP 800-172A Mar2022.
Organization Seeking Assessment	The entity seeking to undergo a self-assessment or certification assessment for a given information system for the purposes of achieving and maintaining any CMMC Status. The term OSA includes all Organizations Seeking Certification (OSCs).
Organization Seeking Certification	Means the entity seeking to undergo a certification assessment for a given information system for the purposes of achieving and maintaining the CMMC Status of Level 2 (C3PAO) or Level 3 (DIBCAC). An OSC is also an OSA.
Out-of-Scope Assets	Means assets that cannot process, store, or transmit CUI because they are physically or logically separated from information systems that do process, store, or transmit CUI, or are inherently unable to do so; except for assets that provide security protection for a CUI asset (see the definition for *Security Protection Assets*).
Overlay	A specification of security or privacy controls, control enhancements, supplemental guidance, and other supporting information employed during the tailoring

	process, that is intended to complement (and further refine) security control baselines. The overlay specification may be more stringent or less stringent than the original security control baseline specification and can be applied to multiple information systems.
Periodically	Occurring at a regular interval as determined by the OSA that may not exceed one year.
Personally Identifiable Information	Information that can be used to distinguish or trace an individual's identity, either alone or when combined with other information that is linked or linkable to a specific individual, as defined in NIST SP 800-53 R5.
Personnel Security	The discipline of assessing the conduct, integrity, judgment, loyalty, reliability, and stability of individuals for duties and responsibilities requiring trustworthiness.
Plan of Action and Milestones	A document that identifies tasks needing to be accomplished. It details resources required to accomplish the elements of the plan, any milestones in meeting the tasks, and scheduled completion dates for the milestones, as defined in NIST SP 800-115 Sept2008.
Portable Storage Device	A system component that can be inserted into and removed from a system and that is used to store information or data (e.g., text, video, audio, and/or image data). Such components are typically implemented on magnetic, optical, or solid-state devices (e.g., compact/digital video disks, flash/thumb drives, external solid-state drives, external hard disk drives, flash memory cards/drives that contain nonvolatile memory).
Potential Impact	The loss of confidentiality, integrity, or availability could be expected to have: (i) a limited adverse effect (FIPS Publication 199 low); (ii) a serious adverse effect (FIPS Publication 199 moderate); or (iii) a severe or catastrophic adverse effect (FIPS Publication 199 high) on organizational operations, organizational assets, or individuals.
Prime Contract	A contract or contractual action entered into by the United States for the purpose of obtaining supplies, materials, equipment, or services of any kind.
Prime Contractor	A person who has entered into a prime contract with the United States.

Privileged Account	A system account with the authorizations of a privileged user.
Privileged User	A user who is authorized (and therefore, trusted) to perform security-relevant functions that ordinary users are not authorized to perform.
Privity of Contract	The privity of contract rule means that only the parties to a contract can acquire rights under it or have obligations imposed upon them under it, even if the contract was created to give that party a benefit.
Process, Store, or Transmit	Data can be used by an asset (*e.g.*, accessed, entered, edited, generated, manipulated, or printed); data is inactive or at rest on an asset (*e.g.*, located on electronic media, in system component memory, or in physical format such as paper documents); or data is being transferred from one asset to another asset (*e.g.*, data in transit using physical or digital transport methods).
Records	The recordings (automated and/or manual) of evidence of activities performed or results achieved (e.g., forms, reports, test results) that serve as a basis for verifying that the organization and the system are performing as intended. Also used to refer to units of related data fields (i.e., groups of data fields that can be accessed by a program and that contain a complete set of information on particular items).
Remote Access	Access to an organizational system by a user (or a process acting on behalf of a user) communicating through an external network (e.g., the internet). Remote access methods include dial-up, broadband, and wireless.
Remote Maintenance	Maintenance activities conducted by individuals communicating through an external network (e.g., the internet).
Replay Resistance	Protection against the capture of transmitted authentication or access control information and its subsequent retransmission with the intent of producing an unauthorized effect or gaining unauthorized access.
Restricted Information Systems	Systems (and associated IT components comprising the system) that are configured based on government requirements (*e.g.*, connected to something that was required to support a functional requirement) and are used to support a contract (*e.g.*, fielded systems, obsolete

	systems, and product deliverable replicas).
Risk	A measure of the extent to which an entity is threatened by a potential circumstance or event and typically is a function of: (i) the adverse impact, or magnitude of harm, that would arise if the circumstance or event occurs; and (ii) the likelihood of occurrence.
Risk Assessment	The process of identifying risks to organizational operations (including mission, functions, image, reputation), organizational assets, individuals, other organizations, and the Nation, resulting from the operation of a system. Risk Assessment is part of risk management, incorporates threat and vulnerability analyses, and considers mitigations provided by security controls planned or in place. Synonymous with risk analysis, as defined in NIST SP 800-39 Mar2011.
Sanitization	Actions taken to render data written on media unrecoverable by ordinary and — for some forms of sanitization — extraordinary means. A process to remove information from media such that data recovery is not possible, including the removal of all classified labels, markings, and activity logs.
Security	A condition that results from the establishment and maintenance of protective measures that enable an organization to perform its mission or critical functions despite risks posed by threats to its use of systems. Protective measures may involve a combination of deterrence, avoidance, prevention, detection, recovery, and correction that should form part of the organization's risk management approach.
Security Assessment	See *security control assessment.*
Security Control	The safeguards or countermeasures prescribed for an information system or an organization to protect the confidentiality, integrity, and availability of the system and its information.
Security Control Assessment	The testing or evaluation of security controls to determine the extent to which the controls are implemented correctly, operating as intended, and producing the desired outcome with respect to meeting the security requirements for an

	information system or organization.
Security Domain	A domain that implements a security policy and is administered by a single authority.
Security Functions	The hardware, software, or firmware of the system responsible for enforcing the system security policy and supporting the isolation of code and data on which the protection is based.
Security Protection Assets	Assets providing security functions or capabilities for the OSA's CMMC Assessment Scope.
Security Protection Data	Data stored or processed by Security Protection Assets (SPA) that are used to protect an OSC's assessed environment. SPD is security relevant information and includes but is not limited to: configuration data required to operate an SPA, log files generated by or ingested by an SPA, data related to the configuration or vulnerability status of in-scope assets, and passwords that grant access to the in-scope environment.
Security Requirement	A requirement levied on a system or an organization that is derived from applicable laws, Executive Orders, directives, regulations, policies, standards, procedures, or mission/business needs to ensure the confidentiality, integrity, and availability of information that is being processed, stored, or transmitted.
Sensitive Information	Non-public, unclassified information. This term includes both FCI and CUI when discussing the government's sensitive information.
Shared Responsibility	A shared responsibility is one where both the organization and the external service provider (ESP) contribute to the implementation and maintenance of a control or security requirement. Each party has defined, complementary roles, and full compliance can only be achieved when both sides fulfill their respective obligations as documented in the Customer Responsibility Matrix (CRM).
Shared Responsibility Matrix (SRM)	No longer used in 32 CFR Part 170. See description of Customer Responsibility Matrix (SRM).

Specialized Assets	Types of assets considered specialized assets for CMMC: Government Furnished Equipment, Internet of Things (IoT) or Industrial Internet of Things (IIoT), Operational Technology (OT), Restricted Information Systems, and Test Equipment.
Subcontract	Means a contract or contractual action entered into by a prime contractor or subcontractor for the purpose of obtaining supplies, materials, equipment, or services of any kind under a prime contract
Subcontractor	(1) Means any person, other than the prime contractor, who offers to furnish or furnishes any supplies, materials, equipment, or services of any kind under a prime contract or a subcontract entered into in connection with such prime contract; and (2) Includes any person who offers to furnish or furnishes general supplies to the prime contractor or a higher tier subcontractor.
Supervisory Control and Data Acquisition	A generic name for a computerized system that is capable of gathering and processing data and applying operational controls over long distances. Typical uses include power transmission and distribution and pipeline systems. SCADA was designed for the unique communication challenges (e.g., delays, data integrity) posed by the various media that must be used, such as phone lines, microwave, and satellite. Usually shared rather than dedicated, as defined in NIST SP 800-82r3.
Supplier Risk Score	Provides DoD procurement specialists with a composite score that considers each supplier's performance in the areas of product delivery and quality.
Supply Chain	Linked set of resources and processes between and among multiple tiers of organizations, each of which is an acquirer, that begins with the sourcing of products and services and extends through their life cycle.
System	See *information system*.
System Component	A discrete identifiable information technology asset that represents a building block of a system and may include hardware, software, and firmware.
System Security Plan	The formal document that provides an overview of the security requirements for an information system or an information security program and describes the security

	controls in place or planned for meeting those requirements. The system security plan describes the system components that are included within the system, the environment in which the system operates, how the security requirements are implemented, and the relationships with or connections to other systems, as defined in NIST SP 800-53 R5.
System Service	A capability provided by a system that facilitates information processing, storage, or transmission.
Temporary Deficiency	A condition where remediation of a discovered deficiency is feasible, and a known fix is available or is in process. The deficiency must be documented in an operational plan of action. A temporary deficiency is not based on an \`in progress' initial implementation of a CMMC security requirement but arises after implementation. A temporary deficiency may apply during the initial implementation of a security requirement if, during roll-out, specific issues with a very limited subset of equipment is discovered that must be separately addressed. There is no standard duration for which a temporary deficiency may be active. For example, FIPS-validated cryptography that requires a patch and the patched version is no longer the validated version may be a temporary deficiency.
Test Equipment	Hardware and/or associated IT components used in the testing of products, system components, and contract deliverables.
Threat	Any circumstance or event with the potential to adversely impact organizational operations, organizational assets, individuals, other organizations, or the Nation through a system via unauthorized access, destruction, disclosure, modification of information, and/or denial of service.
User	An individual or (system) process acting on behalf of an individual that is authorized to access a system.

* Curated from 32 CFR 170, NIST SP 800-171 Rev. 2, the NARA CUI Glossary, and other sources.

CMMC – IT IS NO LONGER "IF", BUT "WHEN".

Here is what you need to know:

- CMMC requirements will show up in DoD contracts on November 10, 2025.
- You need to start your CMMC journey today.
- Although self-certification is allowed during the first year, DoD reserves the right to impose C3PAO certification requirements as part of any contract.
- Prime contractors are risk averse; they want their subcontractors and suppliers CMMC certified ASAP.
- Your company is at risk of missing out on valuable contracts if you do not act now.
- Need help? Over 275 partners, including several Cyber AB C3PAOs, trust the FutureFeed platform to efficiently deliver secure, compliant services to their clients.
- Over 1,200 government contractors just like you are on the fast-track to CMMC compliance using FutureFeed.
- Visit https://FutureFeed.co to stay up to date with changes to CMMC, find a FutureFeed partner who can help accelerate your CMMC journey, learn how your company can benefit from using the FutureFeed platform, and much more.

Attain. Maintain. **Prove it ANYTIME.**

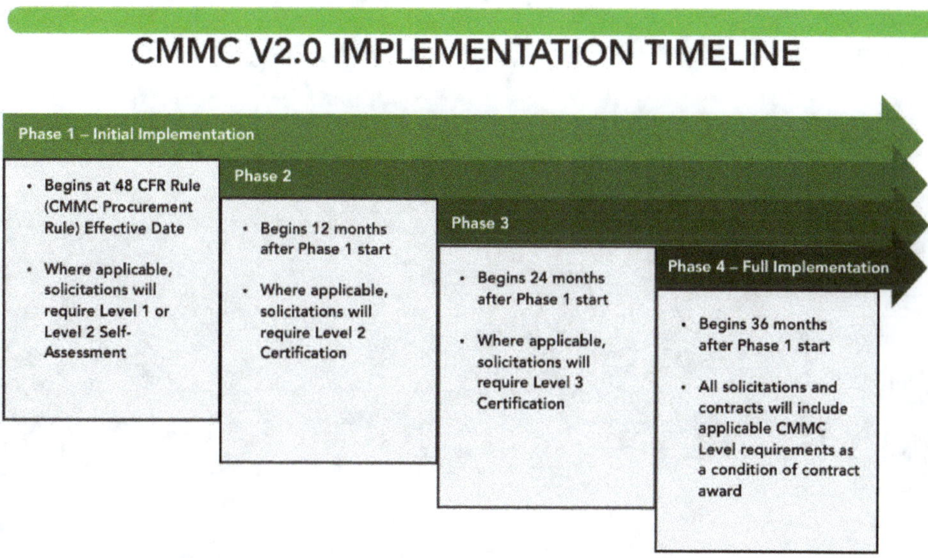

www.ingramcontent.com/pod-product-compliance
Lightning Source LLC
LaVergne TN
LVHW022054200926
848481LV00003B/913

* 9 7 9 8 9 9 2 4 6 3 3 2 3 *